Burying the Sword

Confronting Jihadism
with Interfaith Education

GERALD GRUDZEN

co-authors: Fatih Akdogan and Martin Olando

authorHOUSE

AuthorHouse™
1663 Liberty Drive
Bloomington, IN 47403
www.authorhouse.com
Phone: 1 (800) 839-8640

Published by AuthorHouse 07/25/2017

ISBN: 978-1-5246-6843-3 (sc)
ISBN: 978-1-5246-6842-6 (e)

Contents

Introduction

Over the past decade the growth of international jihadist groups has culminated in the explosion of terrorist attacks in the Middle East, Europe, Africa and some even in the United States. As we enter the new year of 2017 Western nations have often become paralyzed and reactionary to these terrorist incidents. Right wing movements have exploited these incidents and used the fear that they engender to impose draconian measures against immigrant populations and stereotyping of Muslim populations particularly within Muslim majority nations. Even though some political and religious leaders have spoken out against these measures, repressive measures have gained traction in recent elections in Europe and the United States. Themes for this book emerged out of interfaith experiences that my wife and I have had in South Asia (Bangladesh), the Middle East (Egypt and Turkey), Africa (Kenya) and the United States, beginning in 2005.

After the tragic events of 9/11 I focused a lot of my research and teaching on the relationship of Christianity and Islam over the centuries beginning with the period in which Western Civilization was formed during the Middle Ages. I collaborated with a Muslim scholar, Doctor Shamsur Rahman of Bangladesh in the development of a historical analysis of the medieval intellectual curriculum that drew much of its philosophical and scientific foundation from the Arab world. Our book was entitled *Spirituality and Science: Greek, Judeo-Christian and Islamic Perspectives* (Author House 2007; revised edition: 2014). This collaboration received funding from the Templeton Foundation and allowed us to do research for it at Oxford University's Ian Ramsey

Centre for Religion and Science. Two other books that I wrote with Doctor John Raymaker dealt with the dialogue among world religions around issues of justice and peace and the search for a moral world order: *Steps Toward Vatican III: Catholics Pathfinding a Global Spirituality with Islam and Buddhism* (University Press of America: 2008) and *Spiritual Paths to an Ethical and Ecological Global Civilization: Reading The Signs of the Times with Buddhists, Christians and Muslims* (*Pacem in Terris* Press: 2014). Dr. Raymaker's latest book, *Bernard Lonergan's Third Way of the Heart and Mind: Bridging Some Buddhist-Christian-Muslim-Secularist Misunderstanding with a Global Secularity Ethics* (Hamilton Books: 2016) contains many of the same themes found in this book but from the perspective of the mystical or apophatic way of understanding our present global crisis.

The most formative aspect of the present book came in 2012 when my wife and I made our first trip to Kenya and took part in a major interfaith program in Nairobi co-sponsored with the Franciscan Friars Damietta Peace Initiative. During this initial visit to Kenya we met Fatih Akdogan, Director of the Muslim Respect Foundation in Kenya and now, as of 2017, also Director of one of the largest Muslim school's in the coastal region of Kenya, Quba Academy in Mombasa, Kenya. Mr. Akdogan is a graduate of the St. Paul's University Master's program in the Christian/Muslim Relations. He introduced us to many of the key interfaith leaders in Nairobi.

Following our time in Nairobi we traveled to Mombasa where we met with my wife's life-long fried, Judy Walter, a Maryknoll Lay Missioner working in the largest slum of Mombasa (aka Bangladesh). She introduced us to Farther Wilybard Lagho, Vicar General of the Mombasa Archdiocese and also Chairperson of the Coast Council of Interfaith Clerics, the leading interfaith clergy organization in the coastal region of Mombasa. I was able to offer an interfaith training seminar for the Catholic clergy and religious of the Mombasa Archdiocese at the initiation of our interfaith work in Kenya. We returned to Kenya in the succeeding years (2013 through 2016) for interfaith programs with the Coast Interfaith Council of Clerics (CICC), the Bishop Hannington Theological Institute, Columbia University Africa Regional Center in Nairobi, the Maryknoll Fathers and Sisters and the Muslim Light Academy schools in Kenya.

Throughout this five-year period, we have developed a faculty team of Muslims, Christians and Indigenous religious leaders who have helped us to fashion an interfaith curriculum that we now offer to public and private school teachers in Kenya each year. Our faculty team includes a retired New York City teacher and NYU college administrator, Doctor Frank Pisciatto. He has worked closely with us in designing the curriculum we use in our interfaith training programs in Kenya. Doctor Pisciatto has also helped us to expand our work into the interior portion of Kenya where he has met with many indigenous spiritual leaders and done an assessment of their cultural, spiritual and economic issues.Martin Olando, Director of the Bishop Hannington Theological Institute, has served as Co-Director with us of these seminars. Doctor Olando has taken additional training in interfaith theology at the Cambridge University Woolf Institute and the Hartford Seminary Foundation in Hartford, Connecticut. He has authored the section of this book on the state of Interfaith relations between Christians and Muslims in Kenya. Mr. Fatih Akdogan is also part of our interfaith faculty team in the Mombasa region and authored an important section of this book on the role of the Gulen-affiliated schools in promoting interfaith understanding in Kenya through the educational philosophy of theLight Academy.

The Gulen-inspired schools are located throughout many parts of sub-Saharan Africa and which have their own unique educational philosophy.[1] Mr. Akdogan explains this philosophy in some detail in his paper that is part of this book. Kenya has been on the front lines of the struggle with terrorism. The incursion of Al Shabab into Kenya has been particularly acute in the coastal region where other jihadist groups such as ISIS have attempted to stage terrorist attacks in the Mombasa region.

John Baya, an Indigenous religious leader, based in the coastal region, also has played a key role in our interfaith training program as an expert on indigenous spirituality in Kenya. Mr. Baya is presently developing material for a curriculum on the indigenous people of the coastal region of Kenya.

This past year (2016) we traveled to Lamu Island to meet with teachers and students who have been subject to attacks by Al Shabab militants on more than one occasion. Our interfaith education program provides training for teachers and students to overcome the fear and anxiety provoked by these recent attacks.

We are also grateful to the Maryknoll Fathers who provided hospitality for us during our 2015 week long interfaith training program in Nairobi. Father Lance Nadeau, Regional Superior for the Maryknoll Fathers in Kenya, and Fathers Joseph Healey and John Conway gave us emotional and spiritual support for our work in Kenya. Father Healey encouraged me to write this book and provided helpful comments about the nature of the text as a case study applicable to the Kenyan situation. I wish also to thank the Pacifica Institute in Sunnyvale, CA, an interfaith center located near our home in San Jose, CA. This Institute sponsored a program for the San Jose area on the interfaith work we have undertaken in Kenya with remote participation of Mr. Akdogan and Doctor Olando via Skype. My mentor in doctoral studies at Columbia University graciously agreed to take part in our 2015 interfaith training in Nairobi and you can see his presentation on YouTube, "Islam and America."

(https://www.youtube.com/watch?v=Ui2c9SWU2OI)

My wife, Marita Grudzen, has been an active participant in our interfaith programs over the past five years. She has had extensive experience in intercultural and interfaith dialogue through her career at Stanfor University Medical School where she served as Deputy Director of the Stanford Geriatric Education Center.

See her important interview with a Muslim youth leader, Abdallah Ali Mohammad, from an area of Kenya impacted by Al Shabab attacks in June of 2015. (https://www.youtube.com/watch?v=_1UIUD7ADpI). Father Lance Nadeau, MM, Catholic chaplain at Kenyatta University, spoke about the sources of youth radicalization in Kenya at our 2015 interfaith training conference for Kenyan teachers which you can also find on YouTube. https://www.youtube.com/watch?v=i34yCecpabc.You

can find additional photos of our interfaith activities in Kenya at Paths to Peace Kenya on our Facebook site: Our work in Kenya is under the auspices of Global Ministries University which is a not for profit educational organization based in California. Our web site is:www. globalministriesuniversity.org. We are affiliated with the Federation of Christian Ministries --- www.federationofchristianministries.org.

Gerald Grudzen, PhD
President
Global Ministries University

Burying the Sword:
Confronting Jihadism with Interfaith Education

Gerald Grudzen, Ph.D.

Chapter One

HISTORICAL CONTEXT OF JIHADISM

The meaning of jihadism has been debated over the centuries within the Islamic faith. Islamic theologians have generally claimed that the core meaning of jihadism simply means "struggle": either the interior "struggle" to conform to the highest Muslim ideals (Greater Jihad) or the "struggle" to defend the Islamic Umma (community of faith) from unjust oppressors or from attacks by warring states such as occurred in the Crusades. Unfortunately, various quasi political groups such as Al Qaeda and ISIL have hijacked the term as a violent struggle against Western powers such as Europe and the US and also those who hold divergent theological views such as those found with Shia Islam.

The growth of religious and political extremism is not limited today to the Middle East. We are now living in a globalized environment in which the media highlights the latest terrorist attacks upon innocent civilians in various parts of the world often attributed to the militant groups using apocalyptic and violent rhetoric to justify their actions. Often, these atrocities have been focused on Westerners living or working in the Middle East, Africa or South Asia. More recently the attacks have expanded into Europe (Paris), Africa (Kenya), South Asia (Dhaka) and North America (San Bernardino and Orlando). The perpetrators of these attacks are most frequently Muslim youth between the ages of 18 and 30. The motivation of youth who are attracted to religious and political extremism has become the subject of recent studies, but these studies fail to explore the larger context in which these extremist tendencies have found a fertile ground among a segment of Muslim youth.[2] As we will see in a later chapter, the attraction of ISIS and other Jihadist groups is not limited to disaffected or alienated youth. Some well-educated Muslim youth idealize the life of a warrior in the battle to defend their faith against perceived Western aggression or in the sectarian battle of Sunni versus Shia such as we see taking place in Syria.

The Arab Spring represented the flowering of a hopeful idealism among the youth of the Middle East[3]; Al Qaeda and ISIS represent the failure of Middle Eastern and Western policies to confront the inequality and corruption in the Middle East resulting in the disaffection of the region's youth. Few avenues for meaningful careers are available to Muslim youth in many of their home countries in the Middle East. Some have become overwhelmed by a sense of alienation and oppression leading a street vendor in Tunisia, Mohamed Bouazizi, to immolate himself on December 17, 2010 as a protest against police corruption and restrictive government policies. The Tunisian youth revolution led eventually to the resignation of the Tunisian president, Zine El Abidine Ben Ali, in January, 2011. The Tunisian revolution sparked similar youth protests in Egypt, Libya and Yemen. The youth protests in Egypt received extensive coverage by the Western press and social media leading to the resignation of President Hosni Mubarak on February 11, 2011. The Arab Spring gave new hope to the youth of the Middle East and inspired other movements such as Occupy Wall Street (OWS) which began in September, 2011.

From its inception in September 2011, the Occupy Wall Street movement has been linked to the revolutions and popular uprisings throughout North Africa and the Middle East that have gone under the name of the Arab Spring. This connection is reflected in the official OWS website, which declares: "We are using the revolutionary Arab Spring tactic to achieve our ends and encourage the use of nonviolence to maximize the safety of all participants." [4]

This experience of global solidarity has been one of the hallmarks of revolutionary youth coincident with the proliferation of the Internet and social media over the past two decades. We may ask: why did the

Arab Spring fail to realize its hoped-for transformation of the political, social and economic systems in the Middle East?

In January of 2010 I co-led a series of academic seminars in Egypt for American and Egyptian faculty and students just one year prior to the Arab Spring youth revolution. We had an American delegation of 48 faculty and students from the San Jose area who met with youth and faculty from diverse areas of Egypt at several different university campuses. We held numerous dialogue sessions with these students from diverse parts of Egypt concluding with a day-long seminar at Al Azhar University in Cairo. We experienced, with our Egyptian counterparts, a desire for further dialogue and a search for means and methods of collaboration which actually did occur over the next few years.

Upon our return to the US, I was able to arrange Skype conversations between Egyptian and American youth at two of the academic institutions where I have taught: San Jose State University and San Jose City College. In January 2011, one year after our trip to Egypt, over one million youth would come together in Tahir Square to bring down the government of President Hosni Mubarak. The fervor and intensity of this youthful movement could not be sustained because many other forces were aligned against it. Within just a few years the Arab Spring had turned into an Arab Winter, with the possible exception of Tunisia which did give birth to a new, pluralistic and democratic form of government. Other areas of the Arab world have devolved further into sectarian strife or regressed back to another form of authoritarian governance such as we have seen occur in Egypt. Meanwhile, a new and more violent movement burst onto the world scene called ISIS or *Daesh* which swept into Mosul, Iraq in 2014 and proclaimed itself a worldwide Islamic Caliphate with affiliates in other parts of the Middle East, South Asia, and Africa. It soon surpassed the notoriety of Al Qaeda which Osama Bin Laden (1957-2011) had founded during the Soviet occupation of Afghanistan (1979-1989).

In order to understand the rise of ISIS, we must first see how Osama Bin Laden initiated the global jihadist movement well before ISIS burst onto the world in 2014. In the late 1970's bin Laden affiliated his movement with the Pan-Islamist religious scholar, Sheik Abdullah

Azzam (1941-1989). Azzam was the first major Sunni Muslim religious leader to promote a global jihad against the West and to inspire Muslim youth with his charisma and preaching skills. Azzam grew up in Palestine and rebelled against the occupation of Palestine by Israel. He had become a scholar of Islam at Al-Azhar University in Cairo, the seat of Sunni Muslim learning in the Middle East, and earned a Ph.D. in Islamic (Sharia) jurisprudence. By the late 1970's he was teaching at King Abdul Aziz University in Saudi Arabia where he remained until 1979. It was at this university that he probably first met Osama bin Laden. Bin Laden was a student at the same university from 1976 to 1981. When the Soviet Union invaded Afghanistan in 1979 bin Laden and Azzam devised and executed a global jihadist movement with their initial focus of freeing Afghanistan from its Soviet occupation. Given his legal training and status as a scholar of Islamic jurisprudence, Azzam issued a fatwa (binding legal ruling) in 1979, *Defense of the Muslim Lands, the First Obligation after Faith,* declaring that both the Afghan and Palestinian struggles were jihads in which attacking occupiers was a personal religious obligation for all Muslims throughout the world.

We shall see the leader of ISIS, Abu Bakr al Bagdadi, use a similar type of legal ruling to claim that all Muslims throughout the world must support the Islamic Caliphate and attack the occupiers of Muslim lands. Azzam and bin Laden moved to Peshawar in Pakistan near the border with Afghanistan by 1980. There they founded the Maktab al-Khidamat (MAK) which served as a global recruitment network for Arab youth from the Middle East as well as Western countries and assisted in their training for the battle against the Soviet Union in Afghanistan. It provided concrete evidence that a Pan-Islamist movement could succeed. As many as 35,000 volunteers were recruited to join the battle against the Soviet Union. Bin Laden and Azzam set up training camps in Pakistan to indoctrinate thousands of Muslim youth in the jihadist political theology. [5] After the eventual defeat of the Soviet Union bin Laden and Azzam turned their attention to other targets in the Middle East and the West, particularly Israel and the United States. They had built a jihadist movement with its own flexible infrastructure which was international in scope. The ideological and military indoctrination of thousands of recruits could now be mobilized for other jihadist attacks and provide a foundation for the Al Qaeda brand which they had created by 1989.

Azzam died in a bomb blast in 1989 near his home in Peshawar Pakistan. Bin Laden was now free to exercise sole leadership over the Al Qaeda "brand" and infuse it with his own philosophy and tactics. He did, however seek a new partnership with the Egyptian jihadist, Ayman al-Zawahiri. Bin Laden and al-Zawahiri consolidated their central operations in Afghanistan and formed an alliance with the Taliban. In Afghanistan bin Laden planned the most violent attack against the United States since that carried out by Japan on Pearl Harbor in 1941.

Bin Laden recruited 19 young men from the Middle East (most were from Saudi Arabia) to seize US commercial jets and fly them into the World Trade Center and the Pentagon on 9/11/2001. These young men had been recruited into a a fundamentalist and sectarian version of Islam known as Salifism initially adopted by an Egyptian leader of the Muislim Brotherhood, Sayyid Qutb (1906-1966). This extremist interpretation of Islam fit well into a narrative that Islam was under attack by Western forces since the US responded to 9/11 by attacking Afghanistan when the Taliban refused to hand over Osama bin Laden. It was then followed by the US invasion of Iraq in March of 2003. The emergence of Al Qaeda should be situated in the post WWII period in which Saudi Arabia and the US entered into an alliance against the specter of communism leading eventually to the stationing of US troops in Saudi Arabia during the 1991 Gulf War against Iraq. This insertion of US troops played a part in the birth of Al Qaeda and the career of Osama bin Laden since he felt the stationing of US troops in Saudi Arabia violated the identity of the nation as protector of the holiest sites in Islam, Mecca and Medina, and as guardians of an Islamic theocracy rooted in the union of the kingdom with a Wahhabi clerical supremacy.

No other form of religious belief could then be practiced in Saudi Arabia. Bin Laden was a native of Saudi Arabia and had inherited a fortune from his billionaire father, Mohammad bin Awad bin Laden. When bin Laden left Saudi Arabia to join the fight against the Soviet Union he was able to direct large sums of money to this effort and became a central figure in a jihadist movement within Islam which also opposed the US military alliance with Saudi Arabia. In 1988 he had formed the Al Qaeda organization and in 1992 he was banned from Saudi Arabia. He then shifted his base of operation to Sudan for the next four years. In 1998 he was involved in the attacks upon United States embassies in East Africa (Tanzania and Kenya). For the first time Bin Laden was linked with leaders of the Egyptian Jihadist movement which opposed the regime of President Mubarak. Al-Gamm'a al -Islamiyya, a jihadist organization, began a five- year attack upon the Egyptian government leading to the killing of 62 tourists at the Luxor Temple inIn 1997.

September 11, 2001 marked the historic turning point in the US conflict with Al Qaeda after the attacks on the World Trade Center and the Pentagon. Most of the Saudi and Egyptian youth who led the attack on the World Trade Center and Pentagon had been schooled in various forms of fundamentalist Islam prevalent either in Saudi Arabia (Wahhabism) or Egypt (Salafism). For example, Mohamed Atta, the Egyptian youth who flew an American Airlines flight into the World Trade Center, had been trained as a jihadist operative by bin Laden in Afghanistan and received funding from Al Qaeda prior to his deadly mission, Bin Laden continued this support during Atta's flight training in Florida where he prepared for his attack on the World Trade Center. Earlier in his life Atta had been a member of the Muslim Brotherhood in Cairo where he attended Cairo University. Later he traveled to Germany where he joined a jihadist cell in Hamburg. By April of 1996 Atta had already signed his last will and testament indicating his desire to be a martyr for the jihadist movement, an action which also inspired other members of the Hamburg cell. His will, written in Arabic, was found in a bag that never made it onto the American Airlines flight that left Boston and which he flew into the World Trade Center. Atta came from a respected and well educated family in Cairo but he also showed signs of depression and isolation in his relations with other students and colleagues during his years at Cairo University and in Germany where he attended the Technical University in Hamburg. We shall examine the question of motivation in greater detail later in this book. The theories about terrorist motivation cover a variety of sources--from those tied to political and sociological factors to those linked to sectarian religious groups in which a charismatic leader takes over and controls the behavior of his followers.

We can theorize that the hijackers would not have taken on the 9/11 mission unless they were in accord with the motivation that led bin Laden to found and lead Al Qaeda with his notable connections to the Wahhabis authoritarian and clerical structure which had spread to many madrassas (seminaries) in the Sunni Muslim world. In this version of Islamic fundamentalism all truth can be found in the Qur'an, Hadiths and the example of the Prophet Mohammad's life. Linked with this traditionalist interpretation of Islam found in Wahhabism, we also find a legal structure based upon the Hanbali school of Islamic jurisprudence which is the most conservative of the four schools of jurisprudence found within Islam. We shall examine the spread and influence of Wahhabism outside the Middle East in this book as we examine the growth of Jihadist groups in the Middle East, South Asia and Africa. It is important to clarify, however, that Wahhabism was not the only source for the violent acts of Bin Laden, the 9/11 hijackers and the affiliates of Al Qaeda that bin Laden has inspired.

Other major factors that have led to the growth of extremist ideologies are the continued domination of autocratic regimes in the Middle East that have suppressed many of the legitimate aspirations of the youth in this region of the world. Most of these regimes, particularly that of Saudi Arabia, rely on US military power to maintain their position of dominance. Wahhabism became the spiritual foundation to justify the status quo in which monarchical and autocratic political systems controlled all the levers of power in these societies. This puritanical interpretation of Islam can be traced back to the medieval era and the fundamentalist theology of ibn Taymiyyah (1263-1328 CE). Taymiyyah reacted against the Mongolian invasion and subsequent conversion of Mongols to Islam by claiming that they were not true Muslims if they did not follow the sharia law of Islam as promulgated by Ahmad ibn Hanbali (780-855 CE). The Hanbali form of jurisprudence would later become the dominant version of Islamic law in Saudi Arabia in the twentieth century.

Wahhabism is named after an eighteenth-century preacher and scholar, Muhammad Ibn Abd al-Wahhabi, (1700-1792 CE). The Wahhabi movement initiated in the eighteenth century centered on the theological concept of *Tawhid*, the uniqueness, oneness and singularity of God (Allah). All who did not agree with this understanding of Islam were considered heretics (*takfir*). It is this version of fundamentalist Islam whose teachings formed the basis for the theocratic regime of the Saud family dynasty in Saudi Arabia which began to spread these teachings to other Sunni Muslim communities beginning in the second half of the twentieth century using the petrodollars that flowed to Saudi Arabia from the vast deposits of oil that they had discovered in the first half of the twentieth century. They exported these fundamentalist teachings by supporting the clerical training of Imams in diverse parts of the Sunni Muslim world. The influence of Wahhabism became particularly sectarian as it stood in contrast to that of Shia Islam found in Iran and Iraq. The sectarian cast of Wahhabism took root in Sunni areas of Iraq where ISIS would later originate after the US invasion of Iraq in 2003.

This Sunni/Shia sectarian conflict continues unabated to this time in 2017 as we see ISIS continuing to attack Shia population centers in Baghdad. Following the US invasion of Iraq in 2003, bin Laden supported the formation of Al Qaeda in Iraq in 2004 which later merged into the Islamic State in the Levant or the Islamic State of Iraq and Syria. Through an aggressive social media campaign, ISIS soon attracted thousands of mainly Sunni Muslim youth into its ranks in Iraq and Syria. Sunni communities in the Middle East felt disenfranchised by a Shia- dominated administration in Iraq and an Alawite- led government of Basher al-Asad in Syria. ISIS was largely formed in 2004 at a US- run prison camp called Camp Bucca. Since the US had purged the Iraqi army of the Baathist military leaders loyal to Saddam Hussein, many of these men became part of the Iraqi insurgency opposed to the Iraqi government of Nuri al Maliki. This group of Baathist insurgents seized control of large parts of Iraq and portions of Syria as well. Abu Bakr al-Baghdadi proclaimed himself the leader of this Islamic Caliphate (a theological empire) similar to previous Islamic eras in the early history of Islam (seventh century CE – first century of Islamic era). After the death of bin Laden in 2011 by U.S. Special Forces, ISIS supplanted Al Qaeda as the leading jihadist organization and the architect of a social media revolution to attract young Muslims to its cause either by traveling to Iraq or Syria and joining the ISIS military wing or taking on other jobs assigned by the leadership of ISIS. Even though the epicenter of youth radicalization lies in the Middle East where ISIS now controls key areas of Iraq and Syria, the origins of Muslim youth radicalization must also be situated in the history of European colonization of the Middle East and Africa over the past century and the later role of the US in supporting autocratic regimes in the Middle East over the past half- century. The migration of Muslims from Muslim- majority countries to Europe (usually from North Africa and the Middle East) has been particularly pronounced in France where radicalized youth have moved freely back and forth from Syria and Iraq to France during the growth of the ISIS movement. These youths have been targeted by ISIS for participation in jihadist plots such as we have seen in France and Belgium. In these Muslim diaspora communities of Europe such as France, we find large numbers of marginalized youth who live in segregated areas of these countries which led to a youth rebellion in 2007. France and Germany have the largest Muslim population in the European Union at approximately five million Muslims in each of these countries (Pew Research Center, 2015).

Of the Muslim population living in France most have migrated there from former French colonies in North Africa and the Middle East. The terrorist attack in Nice, France on Bastille Day (July 14, 2016) resulted in the death of 84 people and many injuries. The perpetrator, Mohamad Lahouaiej Bouhel, came to Nice from Tunisia. a former French colony. In contrast to the city of Nice where Muslims are not segregated by their religion or migrant status, the majority of the Muslim community in Paris are located in the *banlieues (suburbs),* an area of northern Paris where the Muslim youth rebellion originated in 2007 and from which many of the recruits to ISIS would occur beginning in 2013. The failure of the French to integrate Muslim youth into the dominant secular culture of France and to resist any expression of religion within French civil society has led to the extreme alienation of these youth and made them fertile territory for recruitment to ISIS.

> Historically this is what happened in France's territories during the colonial era and what is happening now in the *banlieues*. This is why it is almost impossible for immigrants to France from its former colonies to feel authentically "at home" there. For all their modernity, these urban spaces are designed almost like vast prison camps. The *banlieue* is the most literal representation of "otherness" – the otherness of exclusion, of the repressed, of the fearful and despised – all kept physically and culturally away from the mainstream of French "civilisation".[6]

A 2014 opinion poll in France found that 16% of French citizens (probably those of North African heritage) had a favorable view of ISIS. The favorability rating grew to 27% among the 18 to 24 year-old age group. Most of those reacting favorably to ISIS are also most likely French Muslims of North African origin.

> *Newsweek*'s France correspondent Anne-Elizabeth Moutet wrote, "This is the ideology (ISIS sympathizers) of young French Muslims from immigrant backgrounds, unemployment to the tune of 40%, who've been deluged by satellite TV and Internet propaganda."[7]

The Paris attacks have resulted in unprecedented actions by the French government to carry out surveillance of any individual or group suspected of jihadist ties without judicial oversight. After the Nice attack on Bastille Day, the French government extended the state of emergency for another three months. Amnesty International, in its report on the French antiterrorism legisation which began after the terrorist attacks on the Bataclan, claimed that the actions were often explicitly discriminatory toward the French Muslim population. Actions included placing Muslims under house arrest without any charges brought before a court of law. Thousands of homes were raided after the Paris attacks in November of 2015 and these actions will continue for the foreseeable future. It is possible that these draconian actions will increase the potential for recruitment of terrorists for ISIS or its affiliates in France. French intelligence authorities can also implement surveillance of all electronic communication and tap phones without a court order.

The historical background to the relations of Islam and France is long and complex going back over 1300 years. The expansion of Islam under the Umayyad Caliphate of Abd al-Rahman ended in The Battle of Poitiers in 732 AD when Charles Martel defeated the Muslim Caliph. This victory halted the expansion of Islam into Europe and started the expulsion of Islam from the European continent. The fall of Constantinople to the Ottoman Empire in 1453 under Sultan Mehmed II marked not only the end of the Middle Ages but also the demise of the Christian Byzantine Empire which had lasted for over 1000 years. The siege of Vienna in 1529 by Sultan Suleiman I (aka Suleiman the Magnificent) marked the high water mark in the Ottoman expansion into Central Europe.

The historic conflict between continental Europe and Islam finally ended at the Battle of Vienna in 1683 when the Ottoman army commanded by Grand Vizier Merzifonlu Kara Mustafa Pasha ended its attempted seizure of this historically European city in Austria. The European forces were led by King John III Sobieski of the Polish-Lithuanian Commonwealth. The gradual decline of the Ottoman Empire in the early modern era runs parallel with European colonial expansion into Africa, North and South America and South Asia. This fear of Islam in Europe became amplified as the French occupied and conquered large areas of North Africa which had been under the hegemony of the Ottoman Empire prior to the French colonization in the nineteenth century. The 200-year history of French colonialism in North Africa culminated in the Algerian war for independence which finally ended in 1962. French colonies also were dominant in Morocco and Tunisia and the French Mandate after WWI gave France a privileged role in the governance of Lebanon and Syria. Muslims from these formerly French colonies migrated into France over the past century and France now has the largest percentage of Muslim population in Europe at 7.5% of the population (Pew Research Center, 2015) A large percentage of the Muslim population in France experiences substandard living conditions and often is geographically and economically separate from the secular society of France. The battle in France over Muslim women's wearing of the veil in public spaces has accentuated the cultural and religious differences between the majority of French citizens and its minority Muslim population.

> Where the French cherish the neutrality of the public realm, free from any religious symbolism, mainstream Muslim culture embraces public declarations of religiosity through the veil or the call to prayer. France's cherished codes of secularism clash with the public nature of the practice of Islam, a faith that in Muslim-majority countries is stamped on public life, from politics to laws to the wearing of beards and veils, or breaking for prayers in the middle of the work-day.[8]

France also has represented the cutting edge of the rising Islamophobia in Europe which has accelerated with the migration of millions of Syrian refugees, most of the Muslim faith, attempting to flow into Europe as a result of the Syrian civil war. This descent of the Middle East into sectarian conflicts and the rise of Islamic extremism in European society has reignited the "Clash of Civilizations Debate" on both sides of the Atlantic. This theory, promoted by Professor Samuel Huntington in his noted book,[9] has contributed to the Islamophobia that now prevails in Europe and the United States as exhibited in the 2016 U.S.presidential election campaign and may have contributed to the election of Donald Trump as the 45th U.S. president.

The Huntington thesis claims that Islam is not an integral part of the development of Western civilization over the past 1500 years. In fact he claims that at the edges of Christian and Muslim-dominant populations you will find cultural and religious conflict. Despite the claims of Huntington, we know that the Arab civilization of the Golden Age of Islam from about 800 to 1100 CE provided the intellectual basis for the development of the Western universities and Western civilization. Arabic science, technology and philosophy were imported into Europe from North Africa and other parts of the Arab world in the eleventh and twelfth centuries.[10]

Unfortunately, the start of the Crusades by Pope Urban II in 1095 left the impression in both the West and the Muslim world that the intellectual community formed between Islam and Christianity had entered a period of disengagement and even hostility. Much of the rhetoric found in today's emotionally hostile environment hearkens back to an earlier era of history when the Crusades dominated the political life of Europe and the Middle East. It fails to acknowledge the periods in which the major intellectuals of the Muslim and Christian faith traditions cooperated with one another and drew upon the vocabulary and research undertaken by each community of scholars. Even though there was disagreement upon matters of faith, Thomas Aquinas, one of the leading Catholic scholars of the Middle Ages, stated in his *Summa Contras Gentiles* that the monotheistic faiths shared "an exercise in philosophy of religion, common to Christians and to Muslims."[11] Aquinas did show a familiarity with many of Islam's notable scholars: Ibn Sinna (Avicenna: 980-1037), Al Ghazali (Algazel:1058-111), Ibn Rushd (Averroes: 1126-1198) and Ibn-Gabirol (Avicebron: 1021-1058). During the medieval era Christians and Muslims generally agreed that they shared a rational speculative and pragmatic tradition which provided a context and foundation for philosophical, scientific and theological reflection, speculation and dispute.

During the scholarly Golden Age of Islam (750 CE to 1200 CE) the Islamic scholarly world had two major intellectual centers, Baghdad (aka the Eastern Caliphate) and Cordoba (Western Caliphate). Both of these Caliphates drew upon knowledge and research provided by Jewish, Christian and Muslim scholars who were employed at Institutes sponsored by Caliphs of that era. The noted House of Wisdom (*Bayt al-Hikma*) in Baghdad was founded by the Caliph Harun al-Rashid (786-809 CE) and his son, Al-Ma'mun (813-833). Al Ma'mun encouraged a translation movement of Greek philosophical and scientific texts into Arabic which was headed by a Nestorian or Assyrian Christian, Hunayn ibn Ishaq (809-873). Al Ma'mun supported the Mu'tazili movement within Islam which claimed that it was permissible to incorporate Greek philosophy and science into what today would be called a liberal arts curriculum. This effort to incorporate Greek philosophy and science into an approved course of studies by Arab intellectuals started a renaissance in both the Umayyad and Abbasid Caliphates located in Baghdad and Cordoba. One of the primary areas in which this synthesis bore fruit was in the field of medicine.[12]

> (Care for the sick was) a fundamental duty of Muslims, Christians and Jews, and it was the surest path to atonement for sins and to salvation. Consistent with Judeo-Christian morality, the Koran frequently exhorts Muslims to show charity to widows, orphans, travelers and the needy, in fact, almsgiving is one of the "five pillars" of Islam, along with confession of faith, pilgrimage and fasting.... The hospital was perhaps the most conspicuous institution of Islamic charity and became a signal feature of the Middle Ages.[13]

The first medical curriculum in the West called the *Articella* was composed at Monte Cassino monastery in Italy between 1050 and 1100 CE under the guidance of a purported convert from Islam to Christianity named Constantine the African. Constantine was responsible for bringing key medical texts written by Jewish, Christian and Muslim scholars over the prior two centuries from North Africa to Italy around 1050 CE. [14] They were composed in Arabic but then translated into Latin by Constantine and his monastic editorial team.

Most Christian and Muslim theologians of the Middle ages were familiar with the basic philosophical tenets of both Plato and Aristotle along with those of the Neoplatonists and the mystical strains in both

Christianity and Islam. The spirituality of Sufism which dominated large areas of the Islamic world in the Middle Ages bears many similarities with the Christian mysticism of the Middle Ages. The growth of Christian mysticism in Spain drew from a poetic and mystical heritage that was part of the Muslim era in Al Andalus. [15] The decline of Muslim influence upon Christianity began in the later Middle Ages with the intellectual debate over the proper roles of faith and reason.

Two of the key philosopher/theologians within medieval Islam were Averroes and Al Ghazali. Their debate over the proper roles of faith and reason would reverberate down through the ages to our time; a similar kind of debate exists today within the Islamic faith over the relationship of truths found in revelation (Qur'an) and those found with the realm of reason and science. Averroes held strongly to the universality of philosophical truth which might, in certain instances, contradict truths in theology. Al Ghazali and the majority of Muslim theologians saw extreme danger in this proposition for it might put in jeopardy the exclusive claims of revealed truths. By the time of the well-respected Muslim theologian, Ibn Taymiyyah (1263-1328 CE), there were many Muslim theological schools that had been influenced by the Greek philosophical heritage impacting both Christianity and Islam in this era. Ibn Taymiyyah was one of the influential theological figures of the later medieval era whose impact extended into the modern era including the birth of Wahhabiyyah (Wahhabism), a traditionalist form of Islam emphasizing a literal return to its sources found in the Qur'an, trusted *hadiths* (oral traditions about the teachings of the Prophet Mohammed) and the life and example of the Prophet Mohammed (*Sunnah*).

The Wahhabi school of Islam came to be the dominant version of Sunni Islam in Saudi Arabia after the establishment of the Saud family dynasty in the late eighteenth century, as we discussed earlier in this chapter. The Wahhabi version of Islam spread throughout the Sunni Muslim world well beyond the boundaries of Saudi Arabia and the Middle East. With its vast financial resources the Kingdom of Saudi Arabia has promoted the Wahhabi tradition in the schools (madrassas) that teach this version of Islam to many of the future Muslim leaders throughout the world. Wahhabism emphasizes, in Western eyes, a strictly conservative and legalistic interpretation of the Muslim faith. It places an extreme emphasis upon the unity of God (*Tawhid*) to the exclusion of any veneration of purely human efforts toward holiness. In many areas of West Africa, for example, we find tombs of Muslim "saints" that had become places of pilgrimage and ritual spiritual practices similar to those found at the tombs of Catholic saints. These devotional rituals at the tombs of saints became common in West Africa but were also subject to attacks from fundamentalist groups aligned with Al Qaeda or Boko Haram. Timbuktu in Mali has been the identified as a World Heritage Site because of its unique Muslim heritage since the tombs of Muslim "saints" are found throughout this region. Extremist groups have attacked these shrines and tombs as being contrary to their understanding of Islam much like the destruction of Buddhist shrines by the Taliban in Afghanistan.[16] Most of these attacks have occurred by those groups who are sympathetic to the Wahhabis or Salafist interpretation of Islam which claims that there can be no physical or devotional intermediary between the Muslim believer and Allah.

Salafism is another form of very conservative form of Islam that has stressed a literal return to the earliest sources of Islam in the Qur'an, Hadiths and Sunnah. There are parallels with Christian fundamentalist groups that seek a return to literal biblical sources without attempting to honor the possibility of the faith evolving into new forms such as we find in monasticism within the Catholic faith and Sufi brotherhoods within Islam. This version of fundamentalist theology seems to underlie both Wahhabist and Salafist claims that all other forms of Islam are contrary to the belief and practice of Islam. Hence other forms of Islam should be at least rebuked as sinful innovations (*bid'ah*). These fundamentalist interpretations of Islam, Wahhabist and Salafist, would become doctrinaire positions in some parts of the Middle East after the collapse of the Ottoman Empire at the end of World War I.

Chapter Two

RELIGIOUS EXTREMISM AND RELIGIOUS TOLERATION IN THE MIDDLE EAST

After the fall of the Ottoman Empire following World War I, the Wahabi's interpretation of Islam spread to both Mecca and Medina which had formerly been under the control of the Ottoman Empire. With the discovery of vast amounts of oil in the Persian Gulf in the 1930s, Saudi Arabia and the Gulf States were in a position to promote Wahhabi throughout the countries which had Sunni Muslm majorities. Wahhabi scholars (*Ulama*) began to dominate as the exclusive body of experts to interpret Islamic jurisprudence and as interpreters (*Tafsir*) of the Qur'an. Wahhabism served as the state religion of Saudi Arabia after the collapse of the Ottoman Empire and also as the controlling force among many Sunni majority countries. The separation of religion and the state has never existed in Saudi Arabia and it is also true in most of the states of the region with the exception of Turkey. It became a secular state under Kemel Attaturk but still gave a privileged place to Islam within its governmental structure. The coercive power of the state was used to authorize Wahhabi and also to monitor compliance with the Hanbali interpretation of *Shariah* or Islamic law. Most observers of this form of jurisprudence consider it puritanical in nature, largely limiting or excluding many of the rights taken for granted in Western countries such as freedom of religion, freedom of expression or freedom of assembly.

The youth uprisings of 2011 in Tunisia and Egypt, aka the Arab Spring, challenged the authoritarian ideology which still dominates much of the Arab Middle East and North Africa.The conflict over the future direction of the Middle East has led to a complex rivalry between the Sunni led coalition of Saudi Arabia and the Gulf states and a coalition of Shia led states and movements under the sponsorship of Iran, Hezbollah in Lebanon and the Assad Alawite regime in Syria. The present attempts to bring about a negotiated end to the Syrian civil war have met with resistance also from Russia. The failure of these attempts has resulted in the terrible destruction and disintegration of Aleppo in Syria, one of the most ancient centers of civilization in the Middle East. Russia has also entered into this conflict as an ally and supporter of the Assad regime aligning itself also with Iran in support of the Assad regime. The cyber-attacks by Russia in the U.S. presidential election have now brought about unpresented levels of complexity to the geopolitical order of the Western world. The rise of right wing political groups in Europe and the U.S. are part of the outcome of the Syrian conflict which has forced millions of Syrians refuges to seek new homelands in Europe and also in Turkey. Russia's presence in this conflict brings back memories of its role in the Afghanistan conflict in the 1980's which originally started the Al Qaeda organization under bin Laden. The presence of Russia in the Middle East will only aid the recruiting efforts of both ISIS and Al Qaeda since Russia has entered the conflict on the side of the Shia- supported Assad regime.

The assassination of the Russian Ambassador to Turkey in December, 2016, has elevated the role of Russia into these conflicts. Turkey, a NATO member, has supported the opposition to Assad but finds itself caught in the conflict as recipient of millions of Syrian refugees, the result of the Syrian civil war. Turkey has been home to one of the most important educational movements in the Muslim world, the Gulen or Hizmet Movement which has now spread to over 100 countries but which has been vilified by the regime of President Recep Erdogan.

Fethullah Gulen began his own youth movement in the 1970's as a chaplain to Muslim youth in Turkish universities. He was able to inspire a spiritual movement that became part of a modernizing influence within Turkey but also in the Turkish *diaspora* around the world. Gulen has espoused a non-ideological interpretation of Islam which aligns closely with many of the themes of Vatican II *aggiornamento*. Gulen, who now lives in the United States (Pennsylvania) has emphasized the role of Islam in service to humanity and also its unity with other monotheistic religions in bringing about peace and understanding in the world. His movement has been instrumental in forging ties with Catholic, Protestant and Jewish interfaith groups in the United States and Europe where there are significant Turkish immigrant populations. The Gulen movement has over 1000 schools in 100 nations of the world which promote interfaith harmony and understanding. The Gulen educational movement honors the role of philosophy and science in a liberal arts education, and students in its schools around the world compete annually in a science-based Olympics. This movement stands in stark contrast to those of Al Qaeda and ISIS which require blind obedience to the presumed authority of the Sultan or Caliph where literalist education in the Qur'an and Hadith prevails. The Gulen movement is now under attack by Prime Minister Erdogan claiming that it is a "terrorist" organization. Unfortunately, this is another example of ideological, philosophical or theological disagreements turning into a possible civil conflict such as we have seen happening in Iraq and Syria and also with the Kurdish population in Turkey. The decline of civil society in the Middle East and the growth of autocratic regimes only play into the hands of extremist groups such as ISIS and Al Qaeda.

The attacks on the Gulen-affiliated schools in Africa have been largely unsuccessful to date but the danger remains that they will become part of the geopolitical conflicts that have dominated the Middle East. We will examine the role of the Gulen schools in fostering a more liberal educational philosophy in Kenya in a separate chapter of this study. In order to combat these forms of fundamentalism in religion or the various forms of Islamophobia in the U.S. and Europe, we will need to devise a new educational strategy which reaches and connects Muslim youth with their peers in other parts of the world. We now wish to examine current efforts to combat religious and political extremism in Europe, the United States and the Middle East and South Asia.

The Wahhabi version of religious and political extremism can also be understood as a response to the failure of the West to engage Muslim youth in dialogue with their counterparts in Europe and the United States. One of the programs with which I am familiar is the Soliya Connect program. I have been a faculty member in this program that arose after 9/11. College students in the US, Europe and the Middle East are connected with one another in conjunction with a class that they are taking in subjects such as Global Studies, Religious Studies or Philosophy. Students meet weekly over a period of eight weeks in the fall or spring terms to learn how to dialogue with one another and explore through direct communication the actual lives of those with whom they are connected. Students develop a media project in which they examine many of the myths which dominate the stereotypes of both sides of the divide among youth from Western nations and those from the Middle East, North Africa and South Asia. [17]

In Soliya Connect Students develop a critical understanding of how much the media reflects the prejudices and prevailing views of political elites in their respective countries, thus often hindering true dialogue among those who reflect civil society rather than entrenched political position of those in positions of power. The Soliya program is just one example of how colleges and universities can play an effective role in bringing the youth of the world into a level of discourse that promotes peaceful and thoughtful dialogue which unites rather than divides our future leaders. [18] Soliya Connect is a partner with the United Nations Alliance of Civilizations (UNAOC) and it has also created a new and diverse media platform for citizen journalism called Terana. It provides youth from the Middle East, Europe and the U.S. ways to create a new and peaceful media narrative.

Most of the educational pedagogies in the Middle East have lacked access to philosophical, anthropological and sociological analysis of sectarian religious systems. At a recent meeting of the Parliament of World Religions in Salt Lake City, Utah (October, 2015) I met with a group of graduate students from Al Azhar University in Cairo at an interreligious seminar teaching the steps to enter into full dialogue with someone who represents religious views different or contrary to one's own beliefs and practices. I was familiar with the U.S. based imam who was facilitating this U.S. State Department tour for these future religious leaders of Sunni Islam who now had an opportunity to experience the diversity of religions and cultures in the United States. The facilitator told me that these students had never experienced such diversity of beliefs before in their lives and it was overwhelming to them. He indicated that they were experiencing a form of culture shock which left them almost speechless and frightened. I had been one of the leaders of an interfaith faculty and college educational tour to Egypt in 2010 just one year prior to the Arab Spring. We traveled throughout Egypt often with a military convoy but still we felt well received at several Egyptian colleges and universities. We were a group of 48 faculty and students from the San Jose area whose trip was arranged, in part, through contacts we had developed through the Soliya program based in Cairo. One of the most important points in our three week journey through Egypt was an interfaith seminar with students and faculty of Al Azhar University in Cairo. We were the largest American group to ever interact with Al Azhar and it proved to be a wonderful opportunity for our group to dialogue with our Egyptian counterparts. Several of the Egyptian participants came to our hotel the following day for a continuation of the dialogue. Some of the graduate students have continued a relationship with us via Skype over the past five years despite the turmoil that has overtaken Egypt after the removal of President Mubarak.

The revolution in Egypt led to election of the Muslim Brotherhood leader, Mohammed Morsi, followed by his removal after a contested election. The present military government in Egypt has brought about growth of Salafi and extremist groups, particularly in the Sinai Peninsula where a Russian plane was brought down by an Islamist group affiliated with ISIS in October of 2015. The deterioration of civil society in Egypt has been marked by the suppression of all forms of dissent by the military authorities. The youth of Egypt have not abandoned their desire for a free society. That desire brought millions of them into the streets of Cairo symbolized by mass demonstrations in Tahrir Square during the height of the revolutionary spirit on January 25, 2011, just one year after our American group took part in our interfaith colloquium at Al Azhar University.

One of the key figures in spreading the message of the Revolution was Wael Ghonim, a 29 year old Egyptian living in Dubai and working for Google. He had seen on Facebook a picture of a young Egyptian, Khaled Mohamed, who had been killed by the Egyptian police. Ghonim started a Facebook page entitled, "Today they killed Khaled," and it soon became the rallying cry for Egyptian youth and within three months had over 250,000 viewers. He became an iconic media figure in the youth movement that spread via Facebook and Twitter. He was imprisoned by Egyptian authorities but later released because of his notoriety and connection to Google as its marketing executive in the Middle East.[19]

It is ironic that the reversal of the Egyptian youth revolution led to another military government in Egypt led by General Sisi. It has also precipitated another level of violence toward the Egyptian government that rivals that which occurred under President Murbarak. Egypt is a country of 90 million people according to a recent World Bank report. Egyptian youth represent 23.6% of the total population, around 20.7m, and around 26.3% of those youth suffer unemployment, while 51.2% live in poverty, according to a 2015 report that was issued by the Central Agency for Public Mobilization and Statistics (CAPMAS) in Egypt (August, 2015). Most of the youth involved in the Arab Spring were located in the urban areas of Egypt such as Cairo and Alexandria and were generally well educated in the use of social media. It is ironic that the availability of social media to spread the Arab Spring revolution is now being used by ISIS to spread its message for recruiting youth to its violent and hate-filled cause. Millions of youth in the Middle East do now have access to the Internet. Approximately 28% of the population in the Middle East is between the ages of 15 and 29 and have an unemployment rate of around 21% in the Middle East and 25% in North Africa according to the World Bank.[20]

Most of the better jobs in this region of the world are in the public sector and unemployment is often higher for those who are more educated since they are seeking professional employment opportunities. Since the governmental sector tends to be tightly controlled by the party in power, those who do not qualify for government jobs tend to become marginalized and targets for youth radicalization. University graduates make up about 30% of youth unemployment according to the World Bank and even this cohort can become susceptible to radicalization because of limited employment opportunities. [21]The weakness of private sector employment in the Middle East and North Africa is another factor that contributes to youth unemployment and youth radicalization. According to the World Bank there is a lack of investment in the private sector because privileged relationships between certain business organizations have exclusive relationships with the governmental sector which exclude competition.[22]

The Egyptian tourism industry expects a 13% decline in revenues in 2016 because of the attacks by ISIS related groups in the Sinai where many Russian and European visitors vacation. The downing of the Russian plane in October of 2015 with 224 passengers led to a substantial decline in the tourism industry for 2016 which is a large part of the private sector in Egypt. The military government of President Abdel Fatah el Sisi has contributed to the growth of ISIS recruits in Egypt by arresting and imprisoning anyone associated with the Muslim Brotherhood. This Islamist organization brought the Muslim Brotherhood leader Mohammad Morsi to the presidency of Egypt in June of 2012. The Egyptian travel consultant for our American group from the San Jose area in 2010 was a member of the Muslim Brotherhood but with dual Egyptian and American passports. He would be in prison today if he did not have an American passport since he had a role in the election of President Morsi. Most of the officials of the Muslim Brotherhood are now in prison and former President Morsi has been convicted of crimes leading to the death penalty. American reporters in Egypt with whom I have had contact now risk imprisonment or exile if they report on the abuses perpetrated on Egyptian citizens by its police or military. A growing number of recruits to ISIS have come from Egypt in part due to its attacks upon the Muslim Brotherhood and other Salafi oriented groups in Egypt.

The *New York Times* featured a story in 2015 on an ISIS recruit from Egypt name Islam Yaken. He had been raised in a middle class neighborhood in Cairo and attended a private school where he studied French. Mr. Yaken concentrated on body building and dreamed of starting his own gym. He started to have questions about his lack of a devout spiritual life and turned to a very conservative version of Islam espoused by Salafi preachers in Cairo.

> Sheikh Yacoub (a popular Salafist TV preacher) is one of many ultraconservative preachers who claim to uphold the most authentic Islamic values, wielding influence and authority through their uncompromising views. They span a broad spectrum, with apolitical clerics on one end and militant jihadists on the other, but they all share a rigid understanding of religion characterized by an intolerance for the other, especially other Muslims observing a more tempered approach.[23]

By August of 2013 Mr. Yaken had left for Syria to join ISIS after he renounced his middle class life style without telling his family or friends. He became a spokesperson for the ISIS cause through use of social media to promote his new identity and attractmore recruits. According to the Egyptian Interior Ministry about 600 Egyptians have left Egypt to join ISIS.

Tunisia is the one country which has sustained a viable democracy after it led the original Arab Spring revolution of December, 2010 when a young street vendor, Ridha Yahyoua, committed suicide. This event led to a revolution againstthe regime of Zine El-Abidine Ben Ali. ISIS has frequently attacked "soft targets" within Tunisia such as the attack on the Bardo Museum in May of 2015 which led to the death of 21 people visiting the Museum. The new government of Tunisia has promised to increase youth employment but recently has been rocked by youth demonstrators, some of whom were threatening to commit suicide following the example of Ridha Yahyoua. The new government installed after the Arab Spring of five years ago reflected a compromise between the secular and Islamist parties, a situation quite different from that of Egypt where all of the leading Islamists such as the Muslim Brotherhood were either imprisoned or forced into exile. Progress in the political sphere has not been matched by similar advances in the economic sphere. The jobless rate for university graduates has risen to about one-third of those with advanced degrees.[24]

Tunisia represents the fragile state of democratic institutions in the Middle East and the need for economic development to provide more employment opportunities for its growing cadre of university graduates. Despite its progress in removing an authoritarian leader and uniting secular and Islamist party leaders, Tunisia still needs substantial international help to stabilize its economy and avoid the attractions of religious and political extremism.

The growing threat of religious extremism and youth radicalization in the Middle East has been exacerbated by the conflict between Saudi Arabia and Iran over the status of Iraq and Syria. The US invasion of Iraq in 2004 also added another element of instability that has affected the youth of this region. The regime of President Bashar al-Assad, a member of the Alawite sect of the Shia tradition of Islam, has joined forces with Iran to repress what was originally a political clash with the Sunni majority in Syria into a civil war with both sides claiming support from the region's major states, Saudi Arabia and Iran. Pro-democracy demonstrations began in March of 2011 and by the summer of 2011 they had grown into massive protests requesting the resignation of President Assad. When Assad refused to negotiate with the protesters and attacked them violently, the protesters formed their own brigades to take up arms against the Assad police and military.

As of the end of 2016 more than 450,000 deaths have resulted from this conflict and millions have fled the area for other parts of the Middle East such as Turkey and Jordan with the goal of reaching a new life in Europe. The narrative of the Syrian conflict has been used by ISIS to promote its cause and led to its expansion of the ISIS caliphate into Syria in 2013 where it established its headquarters in Raqqa. The brutal attacks of the regime of President Assad on the rebel controlled areas of Syria has led to ISIS's use of effective propaganda to claim that Sunni Muslims located throughout Europe and the rest of the world should be recruited to join battle against the Assad regime. Using a very effective social media campaign ISIS has been able to recruit thousands of Muslim youth from throughout the Middle East, North Africa, Russia and some from Europe and North America to fight with ISIS against the Assad regime and the Shia majority regime of Iraq where ISIS originated after the fall of the Iraqi government led by Saddam Hussein.

The election of a new government in Iraq led by Nouri al Maliki of the Islamic Daiwa party from 2008 to 2014 produced further separation and alienation of the Sunni minority in Iraq. Under the Maliki administration Shia militias aligned with Iran took over much of the Iraqi defense of Baghdad as a Sunni insurgency erupted after the departure of US troops in 2011. Maliki failed to unite the Shia and Sunni faction in Iraq leading to the growth of a new insurgency following the death of Osama bin Laden in May of 2011. The presumed leader of numerous assaults on Baghdad was Abu Bakr al Bagdadi, the new leader of the Jihadists in Iraq.

Al Bagdadi had been imprisoned in 2004 in the U.S. prison camp called Camp Bucca where he assumed a religious leadership role among the inmates there. Al Bagdadi had extensive training as a Muslim religious leader and claimed to have earned a PhD degree in Islamic theological studies at an Islamic University in Baghdad prior to his capture by US forces. Al Bagdadi continued his ascent within the jihadist hierarchy and expanded his operations into Syria by 2013 when he formed the Islamic State in the Levant (ISIL) which merged many of the jihadist forces in Syria with those in Iraq. In June of 2014 Al Bagdadi announced the formation of worldwide Caliphate and gave himself the title of "Caliph Ibrahim."

After ISIS had overtaken Mosul, the second largest city in Iraq with over a million residents, al Bagdadi led Friday prayer at a mosque in Mosul in which he proclaimed himself the leader of the entire Muslim world and that all Muslims needed to give their allegiance (*bayat*) to him or face death. ISIS has honed its recruitment message for new recruits to the Islamic State with a blend of theology and brain-washing techniques. Michael Weiss and Hassan Hassan inrterviewed a number of ISIS members for their book, *ISIS: Inside the Army of Terror*. One of the converts to ISIS was Mothanna Abdulsattre, a media activist working for the Free Syrian Army. ISIS was able to convince Abdulsattre that it was in his best interests to join ISIS. A great number of ISIS members who were interviewed for this book echoed similar sentiments --- and hyperbolic appraisals – of the terror army, which has mastered how to break down the psyches of those it wishes to recruit, and then build them back up again in its own image. Abdulsattr's reference to "intellectualism" may seem bizarre or even grotesque to Western observers, but it refers to ISIS' carefully elaborated narrative, a potent blend of Islamic hermeneutics, history and politics. What he described was no different from the total moral and intellectual immersion explained by Communists who later abandoned their faith in Marxism-Leninism.[25] Similar to other religious cults such as the Church of Scientology, ISIS uses high pressure psychological techniques to break down the defenses of those they are attempting to persuade of their presumed righteousness and sincerity. When someone tries to defect from ISIS they often face intimidation and physical threats.

The documentary film by Alex Gibney, *Going Clear: Scientology and the Prison of Belief, (HBO:2015).* alleges various forms of psychological intimidation and abuse similar to the way that ISIS controls the behavior of its members. "When you meet a cleric or foreigner with ISIS, and he sits with you for two hours, believe me you will be convinced," he continued. "I don't know; they have a strange way of persuading people. When they control an area, they enforce religion by force; you have to pray whether you like it or not. We were all oblivious to the most important obligation in Islam – jihad. They shed light on jihad. Every time you watch a video by them, you are going to have a strange feeling that pushes you toward jihad.'" [26]

As we have already mentioned "jihad" can have many meanings in Islam but its root meaning in Arabic is "striving" or "struggling" and not "holy war" as it is often considered to be the justification for terrorist actions. The' "Lesser Jihad" is often considered the obligation of Muslims to defend their faith and the Muslim community when it is attacked. Similar to Christianity, Islam also has a "Just War" ethic which forbids the targeting of civilians including women, children and the elderly. Only prominent and learned Islamic scholars are authorized to call for the "Lesser Jihad" and only when certain specific conditions are met. In February of 1998 Osama bin Laden issued a *Declaration of the World Islamic Front against the Jews and Crusaders."*

> Jihad is a concept with multiple meanings, used and abused throughout Islamic history. Although it is not associated with or equated with the words "holy war" anywhere in the Quran, Muslim rulers, with the support of religious scholars and and officials, have used armed jihad to legitimate wars of imperial expansion. Early extremist groups also appealed to Islam to legitimate rebellion, assassination and attempts to overthrow Muslim rulers. In recent years religious extremists and terrorists have maintained that jihad is a universal religious obligation and that all true Muslims must join the jihad to promote a global Islamic revolution.[27]

The jihad which Abu Bakr al Bagdadi declared in 2014 hearkens back to the original caliphate of Abu Bakr al Sadiq (632-634) who attacked other Muslims that were considered to be "apostates" for failing to follow the the literal message of the Prophet Mohammed and failing to submit to his rule.

> After the prophet of Islam died, a great number of Arab tribes that had submitted to his rule by becoming Muslims – the word *muslim* simply means "one who submits" --thought they could now renege, and so they apostasized in droves. This sparked the first *Ridda* or "apostasy wars" waged by Abu Bakr al Sadiq who became the first caliph upon Mohammed's death in

632. For nearly two years, till his own death in 634, his caliphate's entire energy was focused on waging jihad on all the recalcitrant Arab tribes, forcing them by the edge of the sword to return to the fold of Islam.[28]

In 2004 King Abdullah of Jordan helped to sponsor what was called The Amman Message which "intended to reject extremism as a deviation from Islamic beliefs and affirmed Islam's message of tolerance and humanity as a common ground among different faiths and peoples."[29] The Amman Message prepared by a group of religious scholars from the major branches of Islam--Sunni, Shia and Ibadi— forbade excommunication (*tafkir*) between Muslims, and stated specific guidelines for the issuance of a valid *fatwa* (legal opinion) within the realm of Islamic jurisprudence. These principles were then adopted by many other Muslim political and religious organizations throughout the world but received very little coverage in the major media of the United States and Europe. The Amman Message was followed in October of 2007 by the statement of 137 prominent Muslim leaders and scholars as a response to the speech given by Pope Benedict at Regensburg in September of 2006 which seemed to infer that the Islamic faith had spread by the power of the sword. The documents, known as "A Common Word Between US and You," was addressed to the major Christian churches in the world. This statement emphasized that the Common Ground between Christians and Muslims is the love of God and love of neighbor.

> Muslims and Christians together make up well over half of the world's population. Without peace and justice between these two religious communities, there can be no meaningful peace in the world. The future of the world depends on peace between Muslim and Christians. The basis for this peace and understanding already exists. It is part of the very foundational principles of both faiths: love of the One God, and love of the neighbor. The principles are found over and over

again in the sacred texts of Islam and Christianity. The Unity of God, the necessity of love for Him, and the necessity of love of the neighbor is thus the common ground between Islam and Christianity. [30]

As the spiritual leader of the Roman Catholic Church, Pope Francis has expressed his regard for the Muslim faith through specific actions he has taken beginning with washing the feet of an elderly Muslim man at the Maundy Thursday liturgy during Holy Week services at the start of his pontificate in 2013. In September of 2014, Pope Francis sent a letter to the most prominent Sunni Muslim university in the world, Al Azhar in Cairo, calling for a "mutual understanding between the World's Christians and Muslims in order to build peace and justice." [31] Pope Francis developed a close friendship in Argentina with a Muslim interfaith leader, Omar Aboud. Aboud directs the Institute for Religious Dialogue in Buenos Aires. Aboud also accompanied Pope Francis on his visit to Jerusalem and the West Bank in 2014. Pope Francis also has emphasized the similarities between Christianity and Islam in his first major exhortation, *The Joy of the Gospel*. Pope Francis condemned the November, 2015 terror attacks in Paris that killed 130 people. Using God's name to try to justify violence and murder is "blasphemy," he said on Nov. 15, speaking about the terrorist attacks on Paris. "Such barbarity leaves us dismayed, and we ask ourselves how the human heart can plan and carry out such horrible events,"[32] Francis met with Hassan Rouhani, the President of Iran, on January 26, 2016. This meeting at the Vatican opened up a new opportunity for dialogue about the ongoing conflict in the Middle East and the growth of ISIS and other jihadist organizations. In a statement released by the Vatican the two leaders expressed "the importance of interreligious dialogue in promoting reconciliation, tolerance and peace." [33] The nuclear accord with Iran announced on January 16 and the lifting of sanctions against Iran may also contribute to a new dialogue about the factors that have led to the growth of ISIS and other groups financed by Iran or its allies. The Holy See may possibly play a role in acting as a neutral mediator among the Sunni and Shia led states of the Middle East. Pope Francis'

World Day of Message on January 1, 2017, *Nonviolence, a Style of Politics for Peace,* emphasized the constructive role that non-violence can play in world affairs and represents the best hope for a solution to the epidemic of violence plaguing humanity. [34]

Many of the conflicts in the Middle East have their origin in the tension between the two major powers in the Middle East, Saudi Arabia and Iran. These conflicts have fueled the growth of jihadist groups aligned with one or the other regime and radicalize youth on both sides of the Sunni/Shia divide. The Arab Spring, particularly the youth revolutions in Tunisia and Egypt, brought new hope to these nations as they rejected authoritarian regimes that had ruled for decades. The Tunisian experience resulted in a successful transition to a new social and political order. In 2015 the Nobel Peace Prize was awarded to the National Dialogue Quartet in Tunisia. It is composed of labor, business and human rights organizations who collaborated in overcoming the obstacles to forming a pluralistic democracy in Tunisia. Unfortunately, Egypt returned to a military regime after the election of President Morsi through a coup led by General Sisi.

The failure of many of these regimes to give their youth opportunities for economic and social development, has provided fertile ground for recruitment by ISIS representatives. Even though it is wonderful to have major religious leaders such as Pope Francis lend support to a process of interfaith dialogue, it is evident that many of the issues fueling the recruitment of youth to ISIS are linked to autocratic regimes in the Middle East which use violence, force and intimidation to impose their will on their own people. The lack of meaningful options for many youth in the Middle East and North Africa has made it difficult to counter the narrative presented by ISIS to its prospective "army of terror." The media campaign of ISIS originated in the Middle East and has spawned many affiliates now in North Africa, East Africa and South Asia. The present policies of those opposing ISIS are focused on military strategies that fail to deal with the root causes of its continued existence and its growth. The Middle East represents only a small portion of the Muslim world although it has become the focus of Islamophopia in the Western press.

The flood of refugees into Turkey and Europe has increased the fear that some of the migrants may be connected to ISIS or other jihadist organizations. This fear of Syrian immigrants has also affected the United States presidential race for 2016. Turkey has taken a central role in accepting this flow of immigrants despite the possibility that some of these immigrants may be ISIS members or sympathizers. Germany also has taken a leadership role in accepting hundreds of thousands of the Syrian Immigrants but not without experiencing an increasing call to limit the numbers of Immigrants coming to Germany or other EU nations. A terrorist attack at a Christmas fair in Berlin on December 19, 2016 only exacerbated the fear of refugees pouring into Germany and raised the stakes in coming German elections now led by Angela Merkel, a key supporter of refugee resettlement in Germany and Europe.

A crucial role for religious leaders in this period of turmoil will be to counter the xenophobic hysteria that caused Great Britain to leave the European Union. It occurred, in part, because of the fear of Syrian migrants coming to Britain. The open border policies of the EU would have allowed anyone in Germany, for example, to come to Great Britain. This type of fear of Muslim immigrants only adds to the xenophobia that also affected the climate of the 2016 presidential race in the United States. A trepidation over "Terrorism" only plays into the "Clash of Civilizations" thesis promoted by Professor Huntington. In order to change the narrative used by ISIS and other jihadist groups to attract recruits, we need a new understanding and vision of our common humanity. It should become part of the social media revolution and incorporated into the curriculum of states with large and small Muslim populations. The negative perception of Islam in Europe and the United States is one of the factors leading to the marginalization and radicalization of Muslim youth. The Center for Race and Gender at the University of California Berkeley publishes the *Islamophobia Studies Journal*. They present the following characteristics for Islamophobia:

Islam is monolithic and cannot adapt to new realities

Islam does not share common values with other faiths

Islam as a religion is inferior to the West; it is archaic, barbaric and immoral

Islam is a religion of violence and supports terrorism

Islam is a violent political ideology[35]

Islamophobia has continued to rise over the past five years according to a recent poll.

> Since 2010, Americans' opinions of Arabs and Muslims have declined steadily, according to a poll released by the Arab American Institute on July 29: Since we first began our polling on American attitudes toward Arabs and Muslims in 2010, there has been continued erosion in the favorable ratings given to both communities, posing a threat to the rights of Arab Americans and American Muslims. Favorable attitudes have continued to decline - from 43% in 2010 to 32% in 2014 for Arabs; and from 35% in 2010 to 27% in 2014 for Muslims. [36]

Despite the best efforts of enlightened religious leaders in Christianity and Islam the rising fear of Islam in the US and Europe has carried over into the political sphere with xenophobic comments by political leaders on both sides of the Atlantic.The connection between Islamophobia and youth radicalization and marginalization will be the subject of our following chapter along with the educational efforts undertaken to correct such misunderstanding and prejudice. Fear of the "Other" has a long history in the United States and such stereotypes have become embedded in our national narrative around Native Americans, African Americans, Chinese and Japanese Americans--and now Muslim Americans. The recent ban on immigration by President Trump from seven Muslim majority countries will lead to new levels of xenophobia within the United States and the further isolation and marginalization of the Muslim poplations in the U.S. and Europe by the right wing political movements in the U.S.

Reference

1   David H. Shin has written an excellent survey of the Gulen affiliated schools in Africa, *Hizmet in Africa: The Activities and Significance of the Gulen Movement* (Tsehai Publishers, Loyola Marymount University, Los Angeles,2015) According to Shin, as of 2014, 35 African countries had Hizmet schools enrolling over 25,000 students in them. In the past few years the government of Turkey has attempted to curtail the expansion of these schools by seizing the assets of many Turkish businessmen who were supporters of the Hizmet Movement expansion in Africa. Despite the attempts by the Turkish government to block Hizmet expansion, its Kenya affiliate led by Mr. Fatih Akdogan, did successfully undertake a major expansion in Mombasa by taking over a school that had been closed for lack of sufficient enrollment. The Quba Academy had been a traditional Muslim school established by an Arab businessman in the 1980's but lacked an updated curriculum based upon international, secular standards. The Hizmet educators in Turkey were asked to take over the school in 2015 and it commenced full operations in 2016 and now has over 1000 students enrolled in it as of January, 2017. The importance of this school is that it is located in an area of Mombasa known as the Majengo district which has been a source of recruitment of youth for Al Shabab and extremist ideologies. Quba school has married a traditional Islamic religious curriculum with secular set of scientific subjects that are accepted as part of any secular academy and recognized internationally. The school also includes many of the same interfaith principles developed in the Light Academy schools which do not teach religion. I have included a statement of the educational philosophy of the Quba Academy below.

1) The philosophy of the school is to bring up individuals who are actually and foremost true human beings equipped with Spiritually (profound) Islamic knowledge and lifestyle but moderate and compatible with the realities of the century.

2) This is the school's mission: To bring up a generation which embraces both Islamic knowledge and life styles; academically competent individuals who are well equipped with modern technology and are a reflection of morality to the society.

3) School vision: To offer quality education for the future generations involving the mind and the soul since conscience is illuminated by both science and religion, and wisdom occurs from the combination of the two.

4) The School combines both secular and Islamic education. In traditional Islamic schools, students are only being taught Islamic subjects whereas we intermingle both. The school has also outstanding academic results and administration that shows the community that one can be religious and successful in academics

The parents are indeed grateful for the change of the management. The madrassa officially launched and its syllabus is known. The school reached 100% capacity in a short while from a prior 60% capacity.

The school is no longer Majengo school now but it is school for Mombasa where we receive students from all over the island. The majority of the students used to come from the neighboring region which is known as the hub of the radicalization. They had no opportunity to meet with other Muslims nor to get alternate Islamic education. The school has created an alternate Islamic environment to the habitat of Majengo by attracting Muslims from different backgrounds. Education has its own unique magical setup to fight radicalization indeed.

Educational philosophy of Quba school provided by Fatih Akdogan, January 7, 2017.

2   The study by George Washington University, ISIS in America: From Retweets to Raqqa, has been released as PDF Online text by the *New York Times*, December, 2015. The URL is https://cchs.gwu.edu/sites/cchs.gwu.edu/files/downloads/ISIS%20in%20America%20-%20Full%20Report.pdf

The social and psychological factors involved in those embracing violent extremism has been extensively developed by Philip Zimbardo in *The Lucifer Effect: Understanding How Good People Turn Evil.* (Random House: 2007).

3   For a discussion of the Arab Spring in Tunisia, Egypt and Libya see the article, "Demystifying the Arab Spring," in *Foreign Affairs*, May/June, 2011. The article points out that the youth in each country who led these revolutions operated within very distinct historical, sociological and political circumstances.

In analyzing the factors involved in Islamic youth radicalization we need to be aware of the myriad factors involved in this phenomenon.

4   Anthony C. Alessandrini, "Arab Spring and New Modes of Solidarity Today," http://what-democracy-looks-like.com/their-fight-is-our-fight/

5   David Commins (2006). *The Wahhabi Mission and Saudi Arabia.* London: I.B.Tauris & Co Ltd. p. 174. In all, perhaps 35,000 Muslim fighters went to Afghanistan between 1982 and 1992, while untold thousands more attended frontier schools teeming with former and future fighters.

6   Andrew Hussey, "The French Intifada: how the *Arab banlieues* are fighting the French state, *Paris: The Observer,* February 23, 2014.
    Retrieved from: http://www.theguardian.com/world/2014/feb/23/french-intifada
    -arab-banlieues-fighting-french-state-extract
    We will examine other factors leading to the radicalization of Muslim youth in Europe and the Middle East later in this book such as the failure of Europe to solve the problem of Palestine's occupation by Israel and the inability of Western nations to convince Israel to demilitarize the life of the Palestinians. Muslim youth in Europe and the Middle East are much more in touch with current political events than most youth in North America.

7   David P. Goldman, "Why France Will Do Nothing About the Paris Massacre: Spengler," *Asia Times,* November 15, 2015. http://atimes.com/2015/11/why-france-will-do-nothing-about-the-paris-massacre/

8   Carla Power, "Why there's Tension Between France and Its Muslim Population," *Time,* January 8, 2015. http://time.com/3659241/paris-terror-attack-muslim-islam/

9   Samuel Huntington, *The Clash of Civilizations and the Remaking of World Order* (Simon and Shuster: 2011).

10 See my earlier study with Doctor Shamsur Rahman, PhD, *Spirituality and Science: Greek, Judeo-Christian and Islamic Perspectives* (Author Press, second edition: 2014). We document in this study the role of Muslim scholars in providing much of the early curriculum for the medieval universities of Europe particularly in science, math and philosophy. For the later period of the historical interaction of Islam and Christianity, see Professor Richard Bulliet's important study, *The Case for Islamo-Christian Civilization* (Columbia University Press: 2006).

11 Joseph Kenn OP, "Thomas Aquinas, Islam and the Arab Philosophers," Retrieved from http://www.catholicapologetics.info/apologetics/islam/thomas.htm

12 For a discussion of the role of Jewish, Christian Scholars in the development of medical philosophy in the Middle ages please see Gerald Grudzen's *Medical Theory About the Body and Soul in the Middle Ages: The First Western Medical Curriculum at Monte Cassino* (Lewiston, NY: Edwin Mellen Press, 2007) pp. 154-157.

13 Dmitri Gutas, *Greek Thought, Arabic Culture in the Greaeco-Arabic Translation Movement in Baghdad and Early 'Abbasid Society)* (London and New York: Routledge, 1998), p. 135.

14 Grudzen, *Medical Theory about Body and Soul . . . Op.Cit.,* See Chapter 1, "Monte Cassino and Philosophical Medicine: Historical Context," pp. 17-52.

15 For a discussion of the influence of the Sufi mystic, Ibn al Arabi, on the Spanish mysticism of John of the Cross and Teresa of Avila, see the study of Charles Frazee, *Ibn al Arabi and the Spanish Mysticism of the Sixteenth Century.*

http://www.jstor.org/stable/3269607?seq=1#page_scan_tab_contents See also Gerald Grudzen's "Mystical Visions from Sufi Writers," Chapter 8 in *Spiritual Paths to an Ethical and Ecological Global Civilization* (Pacem in Terris Press: 2013).

16 Ishaan Tharoor, Timbuktu's Destruction:" Why Islamists Are Wrecking Mali's Cultural Heritage," *Time,* July 2, 2012. http://world.time.com/2012/07/02/timbuktus-destruction-why-islamists-are-wrecking-malis-cultural-heritage/

17 For information on Soliya Connect please see their web site: http://www.soliya.net/?q=home

18 See also the Ibrahim Leadership and Dialogue Project based at Queens College USA which recruits US college students from diverse faith backgrounds to engage with other youth in the Middle East
    Through personal interaction over a summer tour of the Middle East. http://www.iie.org/Programs/Ibrahim-Leadership-and-Dialogue-Project

19 See Ghonim's memoir of the Egyptian youth revolution, *Revolution 2.0: The Power of the People is Greater than the People in Power: A Memoir* (Houghton Mifflin Harcourt: 2012) See also "Spring Awakening: How the Egyptian Revolution Began on Facebook" by Jose Antonio Vargas, *New York Times Book Review*, February 17.2012.

20 See the World Bank Data Sheet on the Middle East and North Africa: Retrieved January 3, 2015. http://web.worldbank.org/archive/website01418/WEB/0__C-301.HTM

21 World Bank Data Sheet. *Ibid.*

22 See the World Bank report, "From Privilege to Competition: unlocking private-led growth in the Middle East and North Africa," Retrieved January 23, 2016. http://documents.worldbank.org/curated/en/2009/01/11409150/privilege-competition-unlocking-private-led-growth-middle-east-north-africa

23 Mona El Nagar, "a Private School in Cairo to ISIS Killing Fields in Syria (With Video)," *NY Times*, February 18, 2015.see also an article on the growth of ISIS affiliated groups on the Sinai Peninsula by Jared Malsin, "Egypt is Struggling to Cope with Its ISIS Insurgency". *Time*, July 23, 2015. http://time.com/3969596/egypt-isis-sinai/

24 See The article in *The World*, "Five Years On, as unrest tests "Arab Spring" model Tunisia." January 22, 2016. http://www.reuters.com/article/us-tunisia-protests-idUSKCN0V0164

25 Michael Weiss and Hassan Hassan, *ISIS: Inside the Army of Terror* (Regan Arts: New York, 2015) pp. 154-155.
    For a more recent analysis concerning the historical background of ISIS and its eventual collapse, see Fawaz A. Gerges's study, *A History of ISIS* (Princeton University Press:2016) Gerges emphasizes that Al Qaeda has been eclipsed by ISIS as the leader of the jihadist sect of Islam but that its "brand" cannot be

sustained because it will eventually not be able to maintain its Caliphate in Iraq and Syria. The eventual loss of Mosul and Raqqa seem more probable now that the US is providing extensive training and air support for the Iraqi military. Gerges also claims that groups such as ISIS fill an intellectual vacuum within Islam today. The security vacuum in the Middle East has led to the "collapse of the social contract between regimes and the populace – this helps explain the recent surge of Salafi-jihadists in the Arab world." (p.292)

26   *Ibid.*, 153.

27   John L. Esposito, *The Future of Islam* (Oxford University Press: 2010), p.48.

28   Raymond Ibrahim, "New Islamic Caliphate Declares War on . . . Muslims," *Middle East Forum*, July 18, 2014 http://www.meforum.org/4754/new-islamic-caliphate-declares-jihad-on-muslims

29   Esposito, *op.cit.*, p. 186.

30   *Ibid.*, p. 188.

31   Jaweed Kaleem, "How Pope Francis' Pilgrimage to the Holy Land Could be a Turning Point in Christian-Muslim Relations," *HuffPost Religion*, May 23, 2014 http://www.huffingtonpost.com/2014/05/23/pope-francis-muslims-holy_n_5380231.html

32   *Catholic News Service*, November 16, 2015. http://www.catholicnews.com/services/englishnews/2015/nothing-can-justify-terrorist-attack-pope-says.cfm

33   *NY Times*, "Pope Francis and Hassan Rouhani of Iran Discuss Mideast Unrest." January 26, 2016.

34   https://w2.vatican.va/content/francesco/en/messages/peace/documents/papa-francesco_20161208_messaggio-l-giornata-mondiale-pace-2017.html

35   University of California Berkeley Center for Race and Gender, http://www.catholicnews.com/services/englishnews/2015/nothing-can-justify-terrorist-attack-pope-says.cfm

36   "Islamophobia in America On the Rise Poll Shows," Newsweek. 7,31/14. http://www.newsweek.com/islamophobia-america-rise-poll-shows-262478

Chapter Three

ISLAMOPHOBIA AND THE RISE OF JIHADIST ORGANIZATIONS

The fear of Islam has a long and circuitous history in Western culture. The trajectory of this relationship spans over a millennium through the era of the Crusades 1100-1300 CE, the siege and capture of Constantinople by the Ottoman Turks in 1453, the Battle of Vienna against Turkish forces in 1683 and the modern history of the Arab world influenced primarily by the the establishment of the state of Israel in 1948 and the 9/11/2001 attacks on the World Trade Center by a group of Arab youth trained by Al Qaeda leader, Osama bin Laden. The relationship of the Western world to Islamic majority regions has had periods of relative stability and considerable benefit for Christians and Muslims living in the Middle East and Europe. During the later Middle Ages the Muslim majority regions of the Middle East drew extensively from Greek culture in which Christianity first emerged under the influence of St. Paul. The leaders of the Islamic Caliphates in Bagdad and Cordova often invited leading Christian and Jewish scholars to translate and study Greek scientific and philosophical texts that provided a foundation in higher learning for the expanding Islamic civilization that had spread from Spain to Afghanistan in South Asia within the first century of the Muslim era (621—721 CE).

In the the eleventh century the Catholic Church undertook a powerful reform movement led by Pope Gregory VII to centralize control of the Church in the Roman papacy and to free it from the influence of feudal lords. The papacy assumed many of the titles and power that had been associated with the Roman Empire from which the Church had emerged triumphant in the the fourth century when Emperor Constantine called the first Church Ecumenical Council at Nicaea in 325 CE. This pattern of coalescing religious and political goals and ambitions would plague the Catholic Church throughout the medieval era and led to the Protestant Reformation, which attempted to separate religion from political institutions and make religion a largely individual pursuit and concern.

During the period of the Gregorian Reform era the Catholic Church supported a series of Crusades against the Muslim-controlled areas of the the Middle East with a particular focus on the recovery of the Holy Land of Christianity centered in Jerusalem. The unification of religious and political power in the papacy was an attempt to create a theocratic form of government in Europe through which religion became the dominant force in society and had extensive influence over the secular realm. The growth of a centralized religious power in Europe was meant to counter the growth of a unified religious and political authority symbolized by the Caliphates in Baghdad (Eastern Caliphate) and Cordova (Western Caliphate). It should be pointed out that many Christians and Muslims in the medieval era did not identify with the consolidation of power in a single autocratic leader.

In Islam we had the powerful growth of Sufi religious orders which often were autonomous in nature and espoused a spirituality which was inclusive, largely non violent, peaceful in nature, and integrated into the base of Muslim societies. Parallel to this development of religious brotherhoods within Islam, we had the growth of new religious orders in Europe led by the Franciscans and Lay Institutes (Beghards and Beguines) that sought to be free of material and secular power in order to live a life closely aligned with that of the Gospel ideals found in the Beatitudes.

Pope Urban II called the First Crusade in 1095 and it eventually led to the capture of Jerusalem in 1099. Another goal of the First Crusade was to free the Greek speaking Christians centered in Constantinople from control by Muslim forces which were encircling them. Unfortunately, the Crusaders, who had traveled from western Europe, were merciless in their attacks upon Jerusalem and killed most of its inhabitants including Jews, Greek Christians, and the majority Muslim population. This attack left a permanent scar upon the body of Christian/Muslim relations that has lasted into our own era. (During the attack by the United States upon Iraq in 2003 which finally ended in 2011, the Arab insurgents who fought the United States referred to the United States' soldiers as the "Crusaders.")

The Crusading era lasted through most of the twelfth and thirteenth centuries. These mobilizations of European Christians reinforced the militarization and polarization of the relationship between Christianity and Islam. One of the key perceptions in the West about Islam became focused on its understanding of *jihad* or the justification of violence in defense of one's beliefs and culture when attacked by external forces.[1] In a speech Pope Benedict gave at Regensburg in 2006, he brought to light the view shared by many medieval and modern Christians that Islam was a a religion based upon conquest and violence. Pope Benedict was quoting from a speech given by the Byzantine emperor, Manuel II Palaeologus in 1391, shortly before the fall of the Byzantine empire to the Ottoman Turks in 1493. In his comments about Islam, Pope Benedict quoted the following text:

> The emperor must have known that surah 2, 256 reads: "There is no compulsion in religion". According to some of the experts, this is probably one of the suras of the early period, when Mohammed was still powerless and under threat. But naturally the emperor also knew the instructions, developed later and recorded in the Qur'an, concerning holy war . . . on the central question about the relationship between religion and violence in general, saying: "Show me just what Mohammed brought that was new, and there you will find things only evil and human, such as his command to spread by the sword the faith he preached."[2]

Pope Benedict's comments evoked a firestorm of negative reaction from Muslim majority countries. One such reaction came from the government of Pakistan.

> Pakistan's parliament issued a statement saying "The derogatory remarks of the Pope about the philosophy of Jihad and Prophet Muhammad have injured sentiments across the Muslim world and pose the danger of spreading acrimony among the religions." Pakistan's foreign ministry spokeswoman Tasnim Aslam said, "Anyone who describes Islam as a religion as intolerant encourages violence. She said Muslims had a long history of tolerance, adding that when the Catholic kingdom of Spain expelled its Jewish population in 1492 they were welcomed by Muslim nations such as the Turkish Ottoman Empire."[3]

An outbreak of violence did occur when Pope Benedict's speech was spread through the Muslim world. Not only were moderate Muslims offended, but extremists attacked churches in the West Bank, killed an Italian nun in Somalia, and beheaded a priest in Iraq. Benedict's allies saw those episodes as proving the pope's point, and they cheered his willingness to "get tough" with Islam: "Benedict the Brave" as the *Wall Street Journal* called him.[4] Pope Benedict did attempt to modify his statement about Islam but much of the misunderstanding about Islam in the West has continued to persist particularly as ISIS has taken over much of the media representation of Islam in Western countries. The counter-narrative about Islam as a religion of peace has been substantiated historically and theologically by scholars of Islam in the United States and Europe. Muslims, however, both in the US and Europe, often find themselves living under suspicion and even intolerance. The Council on American-Islamic Relations (CAIR) has documented numerous examples of this intolerance and even hatred toward Muslim Americans. Anti Muslim sentiment expanded exponentially after the San Bernardino terrorist attack and the emergence of politicians who support increased surveillance of Muslims and restrictions on Muslims entering the United Sates from foreign nations. The United Sates has had a history of nativist movements over the centuries in which various minorities were attacked as not in concert with America's prevailing religious and political culture.

The dominant culture of the United States until the late twentieth century has been White, Anglo-Saxon and Protestant (WASP). As Muslims have migrated to the United States various myths have developed about Muslim beliefs and practices. One of the most common myths is that Muslims want to impose Sharia law on the United States. To date several southern states have passed laws which ban the use of Sharia law in U.S. courts. The American Civil Liberties Union has viewed these attempts as part of a concerted effort by conservative groups to attack the religion of Islam as opposed to American values.

> In a disturbing trend, anti-Muslim bigotry has recently crept into state legislatures around the country. Several states have passed or attempted to pass laws designed to prevent courts from applying Islamic or "Sharia" law, as well as "foreign" or "international law." Some, such as a constitutional amendment passed in Oklahoma, mention Sharia specifically, in addition to international law . . . Efforts to single out Muslims and to advance the ugly idea that anything Islamic is Unamerican are unjust and discriminatory and should be rejected. Laws that single out Sharia violate the First Amendment by treating one belief system as suspect. [5]

The increase in fear of Islam has been particularly strong among evangelical Christians in the United States. Very few of the major evangelical denominations have put deliberate efforts into creating a positive relationship with Muslims in the USA. "More than half of evangelical Christians (52 percent) view Islam as "essentially a violent religion," a new report from Barna Group reveals, though only about a quarter (26 percent) of all American adults feel the same way."[6] One of the leading spokespersons for evangelical Christianity in the United States is the Reverend Franklin Graham, son of the renowned founder of the Billy Graham Evangelistic Ministry. Graham's view of Islam is that it is fundamentally flawed because it is a violent religion in its core beliefs.

> Reverend Franklin Graham, head of the Billy Graham Evangelistic Association (BGEA) and son of its world-renowned founder, Pastor Billy Graham, said that Islam has not changed in 1,500 years and has "not been hijacked by radicals," but is "a religion of the 9/11 terrorist attacks." He said he had not changed his opinion at all and, when looking today at the Islamic State, the Taliban, or Boko Haram he thinks, "This is Islam. It has not been hijacked by radicals. This is the faith; this is the religion. It is what it is. It speaks for itself. "Islam has not changed in 1,500 years", he asserted, and added, "It is the same. It is a religion of war."[7]

Graham's influence among many of the more fundamentalist Christians sets up a perennial conflict between Christianity and Islam harkening back to the time of the Crusades.

The growth of Christianity in Africa has been largely influenced by evangelical missionaries coming from the US and funded by conservative evangelical churches in the USA. They are generally homophobic and inspire fear and suspicion among the Christian populations that they serve. In the five years that my wife and I have worked in Kenya to promote interfaith understanding very few of the evangelical churches have shown a willingness to take part in this effort. Most of these churches are focused on conversion of Muslims to their form of Bible-based Christianity.

One of the other problems that most Westerners have with Islam is the generally low levels of participatory democracy in most Muslim majority states. "The forms of democracy that Muslims develop will not be the same as those familiar in the West. The Islamic world possesses a different doctrine of human rights from the West. In Islamic doctrine rights are given by God that are granted through the Qur'an and traditional Islamic law. The supreme authority is God, and humans are his vice-regents, but they cannot be sovereign."[8] Even though the history of Islam has been dominated by powerful and, at times, authoritarian rulers, the *Qur'an, Sunnah and Hadiths* have served as moral norms to which Muslim authorities were bound to observe and show respect

Reform movements have emerged in the twenty and twenty first centuries which promote various forms of religious and political freedom.

> Despite the challenge facing the Muslim world when it comes to democracy, Gallup polling reveals that majorities in countries with substantial Muslim population have a strong desire for democracy. Most of those surveyed agreed that if they were to help draft a new Constitution for their country, they would defend the right to free speech, "allowing all citizens to express their opinion on the political, social and economic issues of the day." In Lebanon, 99 percent agreed with this statement, while in Egypt and Iran, 94 percent and 92 percent, respectively, agree. [9]

The question of "reform" in Islam has been discussed at length by Reza Aslan in his best-selling book, *No god But God: The Origin, Evolution and Future of Islam.* Aslan's thesis is that major aspects of "reform" are already underway within the Muslim community or *Umma* in many parts of the world. Just as Christianity and Judaism have a broad range of interpretations about the fundamental nature of Christianity, so also do we have a similar range of views and currents within Islam. Since Islam has no central authority such as the Catholic Pope within Roman Catholicism, Islam relies on a number of scholars who are respected for their interpretation of the major sources of the Islamic faith, the Qur'an and Sunnah, and the legal sources found in the various versions of Sharia.

A Muslim's cleric's judgment on a particular issue is respected because the cleric's knowledge is supposed to grant him a deeper insight into what God desires of humanity. Dramatic increases in literacy and education, widespread access to new and novel theories and sources of knowledge, and a swelling sense of nationalism and individualism have exposed many Muslims to fresh and innovative interpretations of Islam.[10]

Aslan claims that jihadists such as Osama bin Laden and other jihadist leaders such as Abu BakrAl Bagdadi bear some similarity to the Christian reformers of the sixteenth century. However, just as the Christian Reformation of the sixteenth century opened the door to multiple, often conflicting, and sometimes baffling interpretations of Christianity, so has the Reformation of Islam created a number of widely divergent and competing ideologies . . . Like puritans of other faiths – militaristic or not – the Jihadists' principal goal is the "purifying" of their own religious communities.[11]

Even though many scholars of Islam dispute Aslan's thesis about the nature of "reform" In Islam, the image of Islam as one monolithic religious body is no longer a credible picture. As Aslan points out, the lack of a central authority in Islam allows for diverse interpretations of how the Islamic faith should be lived out in diverse historical and cultural circumstances. Islam bears some similarity to Protestant Christianity which generally relies upon the Bible as the ultimate source of authority but is often interpreted in diverse ways by a variety of denominations within Protestantism. The diversity of Islam is born out, for example in the way that Islam is understood within the context of the North America.

Muslims in the United States are a small minority in a largely Christian society. They are able to practice their faith in a peaceful manner within a diverse and pluralistic society and abide by the cultural and legal structures of the U.S. There is no movement of Muslims living within the American environment to seek the approval of Muslim legal structures known as Sharia by the local, state or national governmental authorities. Even within Islam there is no single legal structure. Just as Roman Catholicism has had a history of its own legal system known as Canon Law so also Islam has its own legal structures usually found in Muslim majority countries.

There are different schools of Islamic law or Sharia. Within the Sunni community we find four customary versions of this religious law which cover the many aspects of daily life such as marriage, dietary laws, criminal punishments and the proper way to celebrate Islamic rituals. The four major schools of Sunni Sharia are Hanafi, Maliki, Shafi'i and Hanbali. In the Shia tradition of Islam the Jafari school of Shariah is predominant. Each school generally has the same approach to topics covered in the Qur'an, but in matters that that are not covered explicitly in the Qur'an, they sometimes differ from each other. It also should be pointed out that in the history of Islam, People of the Book, such as Jews and Christians, were not required to follow the Sharia laws. This is true even today, for example, in Egypt that has a sizeable Christian minority. Jews and Christians have had special provisions in Islamic law throughout the history of Islam and were considered a protected minority or *dhimmi*. The goal of the violent jihadists is to create a fissure between the Muslims living in Western countries and their governments. The vilification of Muslims can only lead to further alienation of them within the communities where they live and work. Islamophobia is completely counterproductive to our need of engaging Muslims in the United States civil and political life. Tariq Ramadan, one of the leading Islamic scholars in Europe, has written extensively on the issues facing Muslims in Europe and the Middle East. He is particularly conversant on the issue of youth radicalization among the Muslim community.

> To spread insecurity and social instability along religious fault lines at the heart of the West is one of the explicit aims of these kinds of attacks. Commanders prey on frustrated youth (educated or not) and manipulate them psychologically and intellectually (on the Internet or in places often far from the mosque). They sell tales of

glory and of vengeance against mankind and the wrongs of history. Religion is evoked to construct, justify and lend legitimacy to violence . . . Jihad recruiters use religion as a political tool and to defeat them we must respond in kind — with solid and rigorous religious arguments.[12]

The youthful Muslims who become attracted to the jihadist message often over the Internet are attracted by the sense of mythic heroism. So also American youth often wish to join the Marines because of the heroic, warrior qualities embedded in this mythic "fields of dreams." Youth are seeking a profound purpose for their life and not just a job or career. Al Qaeda and ISIS are "brands" that sell their violent ideology over the Internet and attract young Muslims who often lack social and economic connections to the mainstream cultures where they live.

One example of this in the US has been the Somali community in the Minneapolis areas of the United States where a small number of youth were recruited for a jihadist organization in Somalia called Al-Shabab which is affiliated with Al Qaeda. Youth are seeking a sense of belonging to a higher purpose in their lives and they may find it in cult-like organizations such as Al-Shabab which promote a sense of self-empowerment for those who often feel powerless in their home communities.

Africa has increasingly been an area of concern in which recruitment of youth for Al Qaeda and ISIS affiliated groups has continued to grow. There have been frequent terrorist attacks in North Africa (Egypt, Libya and Tunisia), West Africa (Mali) and East Africa (Somalia and Kenya). Most of these attacks were undertaken by youth recruited from the areas where the attacks have taken place but some Somali immigrants to the United States have also been recruited.

Somalia is a Muslim majority area of Africa which has been under a U.N. mandate (UNOSOM) since 1992. It is an example of a "failed state" in which jihadist groups have taken hold but which now find themselves largely controlled by the Ethiopian, African Union and Kenyan military forces. The U.N. Security Council is supporting the military forces present in Kenya known as the African Union Mission in Somalia (AMISOM). The population of Somalia is approximately 10 million and the country is almost 100% Sunni Muslim.

In Kenya the Muslim population makes up only about 11% of the total population of 37 million. Approximately 82% of the population is Christian with the Roman Catholic Church representing about 25% of the Christian community. ("Key Facts About Kenya"). Most of the Muslim population is concentrated in the coastal region with Mombasa as the urban center for this region. The recruitment efforts of Al-Shabab have been concentrated in the coastal region with Mombasa serving as a hub for these efforts, particularly among some of the mosques located in poverty areas of Mombasa such as Majengo district and Old Town Mombasa. Some of the mosques in Mombasa have been radicalized by Muslim preachers who are sympathetic to the Al-Shabab message which stresses the perceived marginalization of the Sunni Muslim culture by the Christian majority in the nation of Kenya. Attacks upon Christian churches by jihadists have been common in Mombasa and the surrounding coastal region. Government security forces have been accused of the assassination of Imams who supposedly have helped to radicalize Muslim youth.

The Coast Interfaith Council of Clerics (CICC) has been a partner with our organization, Global Ministries University, in undertaking a series of educational initiatives to train and equip community leaders and teachers in the Mombasa coastal region in interfaith and intercultural skills for use in their communities and classrooms at the elementary and secondary levels.

East Africa and Kenya in particular have been at the center of the struggle for the "hearts and minds" of Muslim youth. The perception among the Muslim youth is that the Kenyan government is aligned with the United States fighting Al-Shabab in Somalia. United States drone strikes have frequently targeted Al-Shabab leaders in Somalia. Unemployment among Muslim youth in Kenya can be as high as 75%, particularly in the most impacted areas of the Kenyan coastal region. This area of Kenya is greatly dependent upon tourism for its economic well-being. It has been the economic engine for the region and has attracted many foreigners to its coastal resorts.

The attacks by radicalized youth affiliated with Al-Shabab have brought about a general decline in tourism in Kenya but the decrease has been much more dramatic in Mombasa and the resorts along the Indian coast from Mombasa to Lamu Island. near the border with Somalia.

Kenya is an important case study in the issues surrounding the attraction of radicalized versions of Islam for Muslim youth. It is distinct from the issues we have discussed about the Middle East but it is also interrelated with them. The West and particularly the United States are deeply involved in these struggles through their surveillance and military operations. United States drone strikes are an important reminder of the United States participation in the struggle underway in East Africa. President Obama chose to meet with African heads of state in Nairobi in July of 2015 and the United States contributed 100 million dollars to Kenya's counter terrorism program. In 2015 United States and Kenyan security forces coordinated closely despite the fact that this collaboration brought the United States closer to a full scale military conflict with Al-Shabab. Just prior to President Obama's visit to Kenya in July of 2015 the United States announced an intensified commitment to anti-terrorism efforts underway in Kenya and East Africa.

> NAIROBI — President Obama on Saturday committed the United States to an intensified fight against terrorists in East Africa, announcing here that his administration would expand support for counterterrorism operations in Kenya and Somalia, including increased training and funding for Kenya's security forces. [13]

The perception of how Muslims are treated in Kenya does impact what is happening in the areas of conflict in the Middle East, North Africa and South Asia. The globalization of the conflict with jihadist groups has grown exponentially over the past decades. The conflict now has taken on an international dimension and is no longer limited to the Middle East and South Asia. Africa has emerged as another point of attack for a variety of jihadist groups affiliated mainly either with Al Qaeda or ISIS. The spread of United States involvement in counter terrorism programs has made the United States a target for these groups. Al Qaeda-linked jihadists in East Africa carried out their first major attack upon the United States Embassy in 1998, a clear indication that Al Qaeda considered the United States a major object of their violent actions. The attack upon the Westgate Mall in 2013 indicated that the jihadists could penetrate "soft" targets such as shopping malls, government buildings, schools and universities. In April of 2015 Al Shabab terrorists attacked Garissa University near the border with Somalia. Forty-seven students and staff were killed in this atrocity which was the largest since the United States Embassy bombing.

Pope Francis came to Nairobi, Kenya in November of 2015 with a message of religious unity with the Muslim population of Kenya. The Vatican arranged for Muslim religious leaders to meet with the pope during his visit to Kenya.

> Nairobi, Kenya: Pope Francis told Christian and Muslim leaders in Kenya on Thursday that they have little choice but to engage in dialogue to guard against the "barbarous" Islamic extremist attacks that have struck Kenya recently, saying religious leaders must be "prophets of peace" in a world sown by hatred. On his first full day in Africa, Francis insisted that religion can never be used to justify violence, discord and fear, and to tear at the very fabric of our societies." He said interfaith dialogue isn't a luxury or optional, but is simply "essential."[14]

Pope Francis urged Christians and Muslims in Kenya to form a united front by seeking to form a common bond which would counter the extremist violence that has wracked Kenya and many parts of Africa. "Here, I think of the importance of our common conviction that the God whom we seek to serve is a God of peace," Francis said. "How important it is that we be seen as prophets of peace, peacemakers who invite others to live in peace, harmony and mutual respect."[15]

The Muslim leader of the Supreme Council of Kenya Muslims, Abdulghafar El-Busaidy, echoed the words of Pope Francis. He said Christians and Muslims must work together to accommodate one another, and lead the country. "We should not step back," he said. "We have to lead, because we are led by the word of God."[16] The Archdiocese of Mombasa supported the visit of Pope Francis by organizing a caravan of youth from the Mombasa region to attend the visit of Pope Francis to Kenya. Pope Francis followed his visit to Kenya with one to the Central African Republic (CAR) and visited a mosque in Bangui, the capital of CAR, where he met with Muslim leaders. Some Muslims had taken up residence in the mosque after they fled a war zone of this embattled country in which Christian and Muslim militias fought with each other.

> After removing his shoes on entering the Koudoukou mosque and bowing towards the holy Muslim city of Mecca, the pope told several hundred men inside that "Christians and Muslims are brothers and sisters". "Together, we must say no to hatred, to revenge and to violence, particularly that violence which is perpetrated in the name of a religion or of God himself. God is peace. *Salaam,*" he added, using the Arabic word for peace. Francis said his visit to CAR "would not be complete if it did not include this encounter with the Muslim community." The chief imam at the mosque, Tidiani Moussa Naibi, thanked Francis for his visit, which he said was "a symbol which we all understand".[17]

The leadership of the Muslim community in Kenya and many parts of East Africa is headed by a Supreme Council of religious leaders who often are not able to be in frequent contact with the youth of their community. The growth of religious extremism often develops outside the reach of the religious leaders of these communities and is bred by the social and economic conditions found within these marginalized communities in countries such as Kenya in which Muslims are a small minority of the population outside of the coastal region. The growth of the Internet and mobile phone technology in East Africa has allowed youth to access the latest information occurring outside of Kenya including the growth and reach of groups such as ISIS who attract many recruits using sophisticated Internet videos and frequent postings on Twitter. ISIS has begun a recruitment operation in Somalia and eventually would like to get a foothold in East Africa despite these areas being largely under the control of Al-Shabab, an affiliate of Al Qaeda.

> Somalia holds potentially huge rewards for the extremist group. It is a marginally governed nation with the continent's longest coastline and borders three U.S. allies — Ethiopia, Djibouti and Kenya."Looking at Somalia, ISIL is trying to insert itself and then may threaten to move into Kenya," Rose Gottemoeller, the State Department's undersecretary for arms control and international security, said at a roundtable in Johannesburg this month. ISIL is an acronym for the Islamic State.[18]

Al-Shabab lacks the media sophistication of ISIS and it has banned the use of the Internet in areas that it controls in Somalia. As Internet access continues to expand in East Africa the influence of groups such as ISIS with sophisticated Internet applications will probably continue to grow.

> Isis is launching a global online campaign on 20 June (2014) to support the group's operations in Iraq and Syria. The group is initiating a Twitter hashtag in Arabic which translates to #theFridayofsupportingISIS, asking supporters around the world to wave the Isis flag in public, film themselves and upload the clips on social media platforms.

In April 2014, the group developed a free Internet application called The Dawn of Glad Tidings, which automatically posts tweets—approved by Isis media managers—to the accounts of the application's subscribed users. [19]

Internet access in Kenya has now reached approximately 54% of the total population or about 22 million persons. Mobile data subscriptions increased by approximately 100% in 2014 in Kenya. [20] ISIS has been much more effective in using Internet-based technologies than governmental organizations, NGO's or religious groups. ISIS uses the Internet to promote their cause and attract recruits either to Syria or Iraq or to form an ISIS cell such as we have seen in Belgium with the network formed in Brussels. The growth of Internet penetration throughout Africa will mean that the battle for hearts and minds among the youth of Africa will be played out not as much in mosques but over the Internet through sites such as Facebook, Twitter and what is known as the "Dark Internet" which extends beyond the reach of most Internet service providers. Schools in Africa must learn how to educate youth to avoid the pitfalls that come with easy access to the Internet. Facebook plans to provide free Internet access to many areas of sub-Saharan Africa beginning in 2016.

The social network is teaming up with the French satellite company Eutelsat (ETCMY) to launch a satellite that will provide Internet access to people in sub-Saharan Africa. The satellite will launch next year and service will start in the second half of 2016. It will reach 14 countries in West, East and Southern Africa. "Facebook's mission is to connect the world and we believe that satellites will play an important role in addressing the significant barriers that exist in connecting the people of Africa," said Chris Daniels, VP of Internet.org, in a statement. [21]

Social media will continue to be the way that youth communicate with each other across the world and form their own networks and access points to other information on the Internet. A recent MSNBC special on the Internet and ISIS pointed out that ISIS has much more sophistication in the use of the Internet than the United States and Western nations opposed to it. ISIS is also training children to be "Cubs" of the Caliphate in which they indoctrinate very young boys to become warriors and even murderers without any compunction, in attacking so-called infidels[22]. The desensitization of children and youth to justify violent missions and even suicide is part of the ISIS brain washing. This type of global recruitment is now considered a war crime and reveals its apocalyptic mission.

Some countries such as Saudi Arabia and Kenya have developed deradicalization programs to bring youth back into the mainstream of their cultures. In Kenya, militant groups such as al-Shabab and the Islamic State continue to lure young Muslims. To fight back, a local organization has launched a deradicalization program to train imams and work with the affected youth.

> The program, called BRAVE—short for Building Resilience Against Violent Extremism, has reportedly already reached 2,000 young people. For those trying to counter the message of radicals, such as clerics and imams or youth not affiliated with a terror group, the program offers four-day training "modules." For radicalized youth, those who have joined a militant group like al-Shabab, the program takes anywhere from six months to three years.[23]

It is much harder to de-radicalize Muslim youth after they have been indoctrinated into a jihadist world view. Schools and colleges need to develop programs that address the needs of these youth prior to any such indoctrination. Special courses may be required to teach Muslim youth skills in critical thinking; these courses may best be taught from an interfaith perspective to show that Christians and Muslims have more in common than what may separate them.

We need also to address educational reforms that will help to broaden interfaith religious education in the United States, Europe and other western nations thus reducing the prevalence of Islamophobia in the Christian majority countries. The attraction of jihadist ideology in Muslim majority countries will be lessened if western nations treat Islam with respect and appreciation of its contributions to the development of major sectors of the world's intellectual culture in science, philosophy and moral and political theory.

In Europe the Belgian government is now funding deradicalzation programs but these have had limited success because of the lack of training for those working in these programs and often their ignorance of the Islamic faith and culture.

> Brussels – While authorities try to track down fugitives tied to recent terror attacks, Belgians are also attempting to root out radicalization in Muslim communities before it poses a threat. The Belgian government is funding programs that feature community outreach and individual counseling in hopes of preventing radicalized men and women from heading to Syria and Iraq to fight with the Islamic state,[24]

The problems associated with the radicalization of Muslim youth are complex and interconnected with a variety of sociological, historical, ideological and religious factors and trends which have not been adequately studied in Western countries. Most of those assigned to work with these issues have been trained primarily from the perspective of psychology or social work. Such courses of study have been mainly influenced by the secular and academic perspectives found in Western universities which have tended to discount the importance of religious motivations or cultures influenced by the Islamic world view.

Government run programs (in deradicalization) face an important challenge: Radicalized youth feel deep animosity toward the authorities who work with young Muslims . . ." Youngsters . . . mistrust everything linked to the state." said Mahmoud Tighadouini, a 30-year-old Dutch man of Moroccan descent. He said he was radicalized online by Islamic extremists based in Belgium and had his bags packed ready to leave for the Middle East in 2007 when he changed his mind. [25]

A parent of one of the radicalized youth living in Belgium commented on the quality of the program that her son had frequented after his radicalization and attempt to re-enter Belgium society.

She said her son was enrolled in the program from March to November 2015. The program involved some workshops aimed at empowering youth and two hour meetings with a counselor once every two weeks, she said. She said the program "was not adequate at all." What her son learned was "very remote from the subject," Ms. Mazouz said. His counselor was trained in social work but had no knowledge of the Islamic religion, she said.[26]

The failure of the Belgian authorities to detect the terrorist cell before the March 22, 2016 Brussels attacks has been well documented. It is indicative of the cultural and religious gap between the Belgian population and government in its relationship with the Muslim immigrant community residing in Brussels. It is part of the larger question of whether there is a conflict of civilizations between the Muslim world view and that of the more secular Western world.

Samuel Huntington first posed this question in his article and later book entitled, *The Clash of Civilizations*.[27] Professor Huntington framed his argument in the context of a resurgence of historical Islamic values which he felt stood in contrast to those of the classical liberal values of Western civilization. He felt that the Muslim faith had become a civilization identity which transcended the nation state and allowed Muslims to be part of a worldwide movement which was just as important as the Protestant Reformation or the American Revolution. If Huntington's thesis can be considered a correct interpretation about an "Islamic" civilization, then ISIS might be considered a harbinger of this prototype. Those youths attracted to ISIS or another jihadist organization would be seeking a more profound identity within this type of ideology and cultural/religious construct.

> "This Islamic Resurgence" in its extent and profundity is the latest phase in the adjustment of Islamic civilization in the West, an effort to find the "solution" not in Western ideologies but in Islam. It embodies acceptance of modernity, rejection of Western culture, and recommitment to Islam as the guide to life in the modern world . . . [28]

Professor Huntington goes on to claim that the Islamic Resurgence is not an isolated phenomenon but is pervasive in Islamic cultures around the world including among those Muslims living in the West.

> The Islamic Resurgence is the effort by Muslims to achieve this goal. It is a broad intellectual, cultural, social and political movement prevalent throughout the Islamic world. Islamic "fundamentalism," commonly conceived as political Islam, is only one component in the much more extensive revival of Islamic ideas, practices, and rhetoric and the rededication to Islam by Muslim populations. The Resurgence is mainstream, not extremist, and pervasive not isolated. [29]

The challenge posed by Huntington's thesis written prior to 9/11 and the growth of ISIS seems both prophetic yet also outdated. Very few of the 1.6 billion Muslim world population presently identifies with the version of Islam promulgated by the Islamic State. According to the Pew Research Center the Islamic faith will grow at a much faster pace than Christianity and equal it by 2070. The world's population will grow to 9.3 billon; the Muslim population is projected to be 2.8 billion and Christianity will represent 2.9 billion adherents throughout the world.[30] The Pew Research Center has surveyed many Muslim majority nations and found only a very few which showed any support for ISIS, among them Pakistan.

> Recent attacks in Paris, Beirut and Baghdad linked to the Islamic State in Iraq and Syria (ISIS) have once again brought terrorism and Islamic extremism to the forefront of international relations. According to newly released data that the Pew Research Center collected in 11 countries with significant Muslim populations, people from Nigeria to Jordan to Indonesia overwhelmingly expressed negative views of ISIS. One exception was Pakistan, where a majority offered no definite opinion of ISIS. The nationally representative surveys were conducted as part of the Pew Research Center's annual global poll in April and May this year. (2015)[31]

The Huntington thesis has been challenged and discredited by many noteworthy scholars who claim that the thesis has contributed to the growth of Islamophobia in the West. We could argue that his thesis is promoting a self-fulfilling prophecy – the more Islam is treated as a 'foreign" religion and culture the more opportunities there are for jihadist groups to claim that the West is inhospitable and intolerant toward Muslims and hence they must form their own empire of Islamic Faith, the Caliphate, because the West is viewed as a foreign government attacking the heart of Islam in the Middle East. ISIS represents an embodiment of the radicalization of the presumed battle between the supposedly "Christian" West and the Islamic Umma. The Caliphate is now being diminished dramatically by a coalition of forces opposed to

ISIS with the support of the United States military. The attraction of ISIS among youth throughout the Muslim world seems to be subsiding.

> A new intelligence assessment shows the size of the Islamic State force is shrinking in Iraq and Syria — but growing in Libya, a defense official said. The new estimate for the number of fighters the Islamic State group, also known as ISIS or ISIL, is between 19,000 and 25,000 in Iraq and Syria, down from prior figures ranging from 20,000 to possibly more than 30,000, according to a defense official who spoke on condition of anonymity.[32]

The decline of ISIS in Iraq and Syria has not lessened the danger that it poses to the Middle East, Europe and the United States. The attacks of 9/11 were carried out by a small cell of committed terrorists willing to sacrifice their lives for this misguided and eschatological ideology. Recent terrorist attacks in Berlin and Istanbul show the resilience of jihadist groups to continue their attacks despite the eventual loss of their base of operation in Iraq (Mosul). We will explore in the next chapter the philosophical, sociological and theological aspects of Islamic radicalization that have allowed it to grow analogous to various extremist religious cults in the West which brainwash youth to follow an authoritarian leader who promises a form of liberation and communal bliss but which become a form of slavery and imprisonment. The election of a new United States president, Donald Trump, may, unfortunately, provide an opportunity for ISIS to advance its cause because Mr. Trump has claimed that Muslim majority countries and immigrants coming from those countries are threats to U.S. security. The link between Islam and violence is often assumed in the narrative of Islamophobia. The jihadists who sanction violence against the West provide it with a religious justification. Pope Francis has attempted to undercut such a justification in his approach to jihadist sponsored violence such as the recent attacks in Nice, France and Berlin, Germany by his challenge to the Islamic state's insistence upon creating a religious framework for these acts.

> Faced with the Islamic State narrative of Christianity versus Islam, Francis' strategy is to polarize in a different way: religion and peace on the one side, violent fundamentalism and false religion on the other . . . Hence Francis says we are at war — a war of rival interests and powers — but insists that true religion is not involved. "All religions want peace," he said on the plane to Krakow; "it's the others who want war."[33]

Pope Francis has recently expressed his reservations about the possibility of a totalitarian political revolution such as took place in Germany after WWI when Hitler was elected by the popular vote of the German people. The survival of democracy may be at stake with challenges coming from various types of fundamentalist ideologies.

> Hitler didn't steal power, his people voted for him, and then he destroyed his people. That is the risk. In times of crisis we lack judgment, and that is a constant reference for me.

> On the matter of Donald Trump, about whom he was asked specifically, he suggested patience. Almost a year ago he said in a pointed reference to then-candidate Trump that, "a person who thinks only about building walls, wherever they may be, and not building bridges, is not Christian.'"[34]

Reference

1 *Jihad* can be interpreted either as an interior spiritual "struggle" or an external combat with one's enemies.

2 Quoted from the following Vatican Online site which translates Pope Benedict's speech at Regensburg. http://w2.vatican.va/content/benedict-xvi/en/speeches/2006/september/documents/hf_ben-xvi_spe_20060912_university-regensburg.html

3 "Pope", *Fox*, 17 September 2006

4 *National Catholic Reporter*, 9/11/2014.

5 Quoted from American Civil Liberties Union web site: https://www.aclu.org/bans-Sharia-and-international-law.

6 Quoted in *Christian Post Reporter* at the following web site: http://www.christianpost.com/news/more-than-half-of-evangelicals-view-islam-as-a-violent-religion-94804/

7 Quoted in CNSN News at this web site: http://www.cnsnews.com/blog/michael-w-chapman/rev-franklin-graham-islam-religion-war

8 Rollin Armour, Sr., *Islam, Christianity and the West: A Troubled History* (Maryknoll, NY: Orbis Books,2003),174.

9 Todd H. Green, *The Fear of Islam: An Introduction to Islamophobia in the West* (Minneapolis: Fortress Pres, 2015) 129.

10 Reza Aslan, *No God but God: The Origins, Evolution and Future of Islam* (New York: Random House,2005) xv.

11 *Ibid.* xvi.

12 Tariq Ramadan, quoted from *Politico*, 3/25/16. http://www.politico.eu/article/terror-attacks-islam-tariq-ramadan-belgium-france/

13 Julie Elperin and Kevin Sieff, *Washington Post*, July 25, 2015.

14 Associated Press, November 26, 2015. http://www.ndtv.com/world-news/pope-says-christian-muslim-dialogue-essential-for-peace-1247835

15 *Ibid.*

16 *Ibid.*

17 *The Guardian*, November 30, 2015. http://www.theguardian.com/world/2015/nov/30/pope-francis-mosque-central-african-republic

18 *Washington Post*, December 4, 2015. https://www.washingtonpost.com/world/africa/2000-miles-from-syria-isis-is-trying-to-lure-recruits-in-somalia/2015/12/23/7b5f3fa0-a4d2-11e5-8318-bd8caed8c588_story.html

19 BBC Online News, June 19.2014. http://www.bbc.com/news/world-middle-east-27912569
PBS has documented the recruitment of Kenya youth by Al Shabab in the following report: http://www.pbs.org/newshour/bb/how-al-shabaab-is-recruiting-young-men-from-kenya/

20 *Technology News Review (Techweez,* April 4, 2016. http://www.techweez. com/2015/04/29/Internet-penetration-in-kenya-2015/

21 Heather Kelly, *CNN Money,* October 5, 2015. http://money.cnn.com/2015/10/ 05/technology/facebook-africa-satellites/index.html.

22 MSNBC," *Cubs of the Caliphate": Role of Kids in ISIS.* 4/1/2016. http:// www.msnbc.com/documentaries/watch/cubs-of-the-caliphate-role -of-kids-in-isis-657411651738

23 Lenny Ruvaga, Voice of America, March 9, 2016. http://www.voanews.com/ content/kenya-de-radicalization/3227614.html

24 Natalia Drozdiak and Matthias Verbergt, "Belgians Try to Reach Radicals Before Threat Emerges," *Wall Street Journal,* 4/4/2016, p. A15.

25 *Ibid.* p. A15.

26 Ibid. p. A15.

27 Samuel P. Huntington, *The Clash of Civilizations and the Remaking of World Order* (New York: Touchstone Press, 1997).

28 *Ibid.,* 108-109.

29 *Ibid.* 109.

30 Bill Chapell, *NPR,* August 2, 2015. http://www.npr.org/sections/thetwo-way/2015/04/02/397042004/muslim-population-will-surpass-christians -this-century-pew-says

31 *Pew Research Center,* November 17, 2015. http://www.pewresearch.org/fact-tank/2015/11/17/in-nations-with-significant-muslim-populations-much-disdain-for-isisAl

32 Andrew Tilghman, *Military Times,* 2/4/2016. http://www.militarytimes. com/story/military/2016/02/04/new-intel-shows-isis-force-declining -iraq-syria/79819744/

33 "Pope Francis' six-fold response to jihadist terror," *Mercatornet,* August 9,2016. https://www.mercatornet.com/above/view/pope-franciss-six-fold -response-to-jihadist-terror/18490

34 The Daily Beast, January 25, 2017.http://www.thedailybeast.com/articles /2017/01/25/where-pope-francis-sees-hitler-rising-today.html

Chapter Four

RADICALIZATION OF MUSLIM YOUTH: PSYCHOLOGICAL, SOCIOLOGICAL AND THEOLOGICAL FACTORS

Recent studies of terrorist-related incidents have focused on the role of the "suicide bomber" since most of the deaths caused by these attacks have been attributed to young men committing suicide by blowing themselves up in highly populated urban areas such as airports, government buildings and commercial shopping areas.

> This attention is arguably justified. Between 1980 and 2004, for example, suicide bombings accounted for 48% of all deaths through terrorism despite its use in only 3% of incidents (Pape, 2005).[1]

A series of studies have shown that the conventional picture of a terrorist as an alienated youth with limited formal education does not always fit into this typology. Most of the 9/11 hijackers were well-educated and had gone through extensive training to coordinate with each other and overcome the pilots and crew of several planes and fly them into their desired targets killing themselves, the passengers and several thousand others located in the Twin Towers and the Pentagon. Initial studies on terrorists seemed to focus on various types of mental health pathologies that often are characteristic of suicide victims such as depression, unbridled anger, suicidal impulses and unstable personal identity. "These findings seem to run contrary to the growing realization within terrorism studies that psychopathology among the terrorist population is not significantly different from that in other populations (Horgan, 2005; Silke, 1998)."[2]

Personality differences among suicide bombers and the general population have yet to to be demonstrated as sufficiently important to explain the motivation of suicide bombers.

Another line of research that seems more fruitful is the role that social psychology plays in the evolution of a suicide bomber. In our Western culture we tend to focus on the motivation of the individual to determine why someone commits a terrorist act. In much of Western literature the person who commits such acts is deviating drastically from the most basic social norms found in most Western nations. From the European and American perspective, the mental state of the suicide bomber represents a distorted and pathological condition which is contrary to any moral justification.

Philip Zimbardo in his classic study, *The Lucifer Effect: Understanding How Good People Turn Evil,* has shown how social factors can influence the way a situation is perceived and how the actors in that situation can create an alternative moral code – what is evil becomes "good" in the eyes of those with power to control their captors through their position of power and authority. In the Stanford Prison Experiment we can see how cognitive dissonance begins to justify and rationalize evil behavior.

> An interesting consequence of playing a role publicly that is contrary to one's private belief is the creation of *cognitive dissonance.* When there is a discrepancy between one's behavior and beliefs, and when actions do not follow from relevant attitudes, a condition of cognitive dissonance is created. Dissonance is a state of tension that can powerfully motivate change either in one's public behavior or in one's private efforts to reduce dissonance. [3]

This concept of dissonance in belief systems does not mean that the "conversion" to a Jihadist ideology is necessarily based on religious concerns or observant behavior. The lack of meaning in one's life can lead to an experience of dissonance. "As the French sociologist Olivier Roy, the preeminent scholar of European jihadism, puts it, few terrorists "have a previous story of militancy," either political or religious. Rather, they're searching for something less definable: identity, meaning, respect." [4]

The sense of discontinuity between the inner life of a young person and his or her external world may be the starting point for youth radicalization. Often the process of maturation taking place in a young person creates an internal conflict between the heroic aspirations that often fill the mind and emotions of most youth as they move from adolescence into adulthood and the existential context of their current life situation. Often the dissonance may not be visible to the youth's family since part of the changing culture of our time is the role of the Internet and social media. These youth are seeking an identity that often transcends the materialistic and pragmatic goals instilled in them by Western culture and Western style secular education either in Europe or the Middle East.

"It is not through mosques but through the Internet that such jihadists discover their community. Dissociated from social norms, finding their identity, within a small group, radicals come to see world events as an existential struggle between Islam and the West and feel empowered to commit acts of horror." [5] The process by which an individual goes from accepting the social norms found in their society of origin and those found within the community of jihadist is often complex and multidimensional.

> Kruglanski, Chen, Dechesne, Fishman, and Orehek's research on the psychology of suicide terrorism is about understanding terrorist motivation. In particular, the authors' concern is that the multiplicity of motivational sources identified in the terrorism studies literature should be subsumed into a simpler set of categories.

The researchers do this by focusing primarily on the individual actor in an effort to "connect the dots" between the ideological, personal, and social motivations for suicide terror and aggregate various motives under the umbrella term of a *quest for personal significance.*[6]

Victor Frankl, the founder of the school of psychotherapy known as logo therapy, developed most of his psychoanalytic theory in the context of the Nazi concentration camps.

He experienced his own struggle for meaning in the midst of an irrational human tragedy that seemed beyond any human comprehension to understand or fathom its meaning for those imprisoned and for their captors. Frankl discovered that human beings will almost always seek to find meaning in seemingly hopeless situations such as he experienced in the concentration camps of the Nazis.

> We must never forget that we may also find meaning in life even when confronted with a hopeless situation, when facing a fate that cannot be changed. For what then matters is to bear witness to the uniquely human potential at its best, which is to transform a personal tragedy into a triumph, to turn one's predicaments into a human achievement. When we are no longer able to change a situation — just think of an incurable disease such as incurable cancer – we are challenged to change ourselves.[7]

Those who engage in terrorist activities such as suicide bombing may be seeking to transcend the seeming "hopelessness" that they experience in their personal lives and view the jihadist community as a path to heroic achievement even if it ends with their own death. Dr.

Peter Barglow has studied the lives of eight young terrorists who resided about Fredrikstad, Norway, who formed a jihadist community in 2012, *The Prophet's Ummah,* which was linked initially to Al Qaeda but later with ISIS or ISIL.

Dr. Barglow uses the stages of psychosocial development of Erik Erickson to explain the behavior of these Norwegian jihadists. Erik Erickson established a psychosocial grouping of normal and abnormal individuals according to age periods. This selection process was used to create personal identity types characterized by alternative personal psychic attributes

> What are the emotional pathways that males with these sorts of mental problems can pursue? such as "trust" versus "mistrust," or "ego identity versus despair." Adolescents and young adults have the alternative of "Identity versus Role Confusion" during the fifth part of Erikson's eight-stage lifespan sequence of normative developmental tasks . . . Identity "diffusion" is the consequence of such choices remaining unresolved. [8]

The question of "identity diffusion" within the parameters of Erikson's theories can be contextualized in Dr. Barlow's analysis by examining the nature of the immigrant personality and the emotional challenges that affect their adolescent children seeking to achieve a new identity within the majority culture of a Western nation. This "diffusion" of identities can lead to what Zimbardo calls "cognitive dissonance." The conflict between two distinct cultural realities can lead to an existential choice about where the youth can find his or her true identity.

> Failure to navigate any of these pathways and the constant trauma of harsh poverty, family turmoil, and peer rejection may produce personality fragmentation and serious identity and role diffusion. [9]

The role of the terrorist cell or group in explaining the actions of the individual terrorist is one that Philip Zinbardo has emphasized in his research. The individual who is not clear about his or her identity may be easily influenced by the terrorist cell which has recruited him or her into its network or jihadist community.

> Typically, people are also unaware of an even stronger force playing on the strings of their behavioral repertoire: *the need for social approval.* The need to be accepted, liked and respected – to seem normal and appropriate, to fit in — is so powerful that we are primed to conform to even the most foolish and outlandish behaviors that strangers tell us is the right way to act. [10]

The Stanford Prison Experiment did show that an individually "moral" youth can succumb to the pressures brought upon him to conform to what is perceived to be the moral norm of a group or organization that has influence over his behavior.

> Philip Zimbardo (2004) says that although we might be conditioned to look for answers in the individual's psychology, in fact the group, organizational, and cultural context is far more important. Ehud Sprink argued that the best way to halt suicide attacks is to study not the suicide bombers themselves, but the organizations that press these young men and women into their last, ghastly service (see Gill, 2007, 2008). [11]

The Stanford Prison Experiment demonstrated the power of group psychology to bond youth together in an enterprise which was discordant with their private moral norms and instincts. The authority of the group and its presumed value as a university approved experiment allowed the participants to override any personal moral compunctions. We can use this experiment as an analogy to the recruitment of youth by Al Qaeda and ISIS who combine not only the power of group psychology but also the authority of a religious tradition to give credibility to a clearly immoral series of actions against innocent civilians.

However, as was obvious in the events that unfolded on the second day, the prisoners came to believe that it was a prison being run by psychologists and not by the State. They persuaded themselves, based on the quip by Doug—8612, that no one could leave of his own volition . . . The prisoners themselves became their own guards.[12]

We can also see that part of the pressure to conform may come from the authority found within Stanford University itself as a premier institution of higher learning in the US and in the world.

Academic, political and religious institutions can be a powerful influence upon the identity and motivation of those who embrace the sociological and epistemological validity of these institutions to compel acquiescence to their behavioral norms even when they seem to be contrary to their private moral codes or behavior. Youth who are recruited to terrorist groups often lack clear understanding of what attracts them to join a jihadist organization. We have seen that it is often the lack of a coherent identity within the societies in which they live because they are often first generation members of that society. In other cases, such as in Palestine, a whole culture can develop in which suicide bombers are glorified in the popular culture of communities living under oppressive circumstances. In the case of suicide bombers within European society we usually find that the cells which promote this type of activity are located within marginalized communities such as we found in the Molenbeek region of Belgium where most of the recent suicide bombers in France and Belgium originated. The culture of certain regions of Europe has splintered into seeding grounds for Islamic extremist nfluences.

Molenbeek is one of the poorest regions in Belgium with an unemployment rate for youth under 25 at over 35%. Europe has allowed ghettos to grow in many of its urban areas. Many of these ghettos attract extremist Muslim clerics who indoctrinate youth who are themselves vulnerable to extremism because of their isolation from the mainstreams of European culture.

> But Molenbeek is just the most acute manifestation of a European failure. The large-scale immigration from Turkey and North Africa that began a half-century ago at a time of economic boom has — at a time of economic stagnation — led to near-ghettos in or around many European cities where the jobless descendants of those migrants are sometimes radicalized by Wahhabi clerics. [13]

The divide between the mainstream European culture and that of the minority Arab cultures has only grown more acute over the past decade. The lack of stability in many parts of the Middle East, South Asia and North Africa does have consequences for Europe and the rest of the world.

Many of the youth attracted to jihadist organizations are often not acting in an irrational manner or with immoral intentions according to their own social norms. The context for many of the youth in Europe is the result of their communities failing to integrate into the larger European society. Recent debates in Great Britain have centered around whether Muslim communities in the UK have created a "state within a state." Trevor Philips, former head of the Equality and Human Rights Commission, has claimed that a sufficiently significant percentage (23%) of Muslims in the UK wish to live within the context of *Shariah* law if it were allowed to govern their communities. Even though many commentators suggest that the data was skewed, it does point out that there are major cultural differences among those Muslims coming from socially conservative countries such as Pakistan or Bangladesh to the UK. The problem with these types of surveys is that they reinforce the views of those who are intolerant toward the Islamic faith and further alienate many of the Muslim youth who are already outside the mainstream of European society. The growth of Islamophobia in Great Britain has been well documented.

In 2011, 75 percent viewed Islam as the most violent religion and 43 percent saw Muslims as fanatical. Worryingly, large segments of British society today believe that Muslims possess dual loyalties and the number of those who perceive Islam as a threat to Western liberal democracy has risen sharply. Iislamophobia is becoming increasingly institutionalised.[14]

The growth of anti-Muslim sentiment in Western countries does help to fuel the perception among Muslim youth in diverse areas of the world that there is a concerted effort to demonize Islam and portray it in an unfavourable way. A counter narrative to the Clash of Civilizations thesis has been the Alliance of Civilizations (UNAOC) initiative begun in 2002 and now under the auspices of the United Nations. One of the key supporters and members of the UNAOC advisory council (High Level Group) has been the scholar of world religions and a British citizen, Karen Armstrong. Armstrong combats the image of Islam as a violent religion in many of her writings and in public appearances such as the Parliament of World Religions meeting this past November in Salt Lake City, Utah. Armstrong argues that the "Clash" of Civilizations is really within religions themselves and is not limited to Islam and Christianity. In one of her books, *The Battle for God*, she has documented the rise of fundamentalism in three monotheistic religions over the past 500 years as modernity took hold in the Western world.[15] In Armstrong's latest book, *Fields of Blood*, she points out that that history of the Middle East has been plagued by both colonialism and secularism which themselves were bloody and violent and had little to do with religion.

> As the Europeans dismantled their empires and left the region, they ceded power to the precolonial ruling classes, which were so embedded in the old aristocratic ethos that they were incapable of modernization. They were usually deposed in coups organized by reform-minded army officers, who were the only commoners to receive a Western style education. Reza Khan in

Iran (1921), Colonel Adib Shissak in Syria (1949), and Gamal Abdal-Nassar in Egypt (1952) . . . . Indeed, these secularizing rulers effectively terrorized their subjects by tearing down familiar institutions so that their world became unrecognizable.[16]

The attempted secularization of the Middle East by military style governments led to a reaction against these governments by fundamentalist groups that appealed to political Islam as the answer to a crisis that these societies were experiencing after they attained independence from European powers in the twentieth century. The ascendancy of the British in Egypt in the nineteenth century had left Egypt without a clear path to modernity and integration of traditional Islamic values into the Egyptian society. Some of the key reform attempts had taken place at Al-Azhar University, the most important center for Sunni Islam in the world. "Mohammad Abdu (1849-1905), Sheikh of Al-Azhar, suggested that modern legal and constitutional arrangements should be linked to traditional Islamic norms that would make them comprehensible." [17] A schoolteacher in Egypt, Hassan al-Banna (1906-1949 became the founder of the Muslim Brotherhood in 1928 as an effort to unite traditional Muslim cultural and legal values with the modernizing trends imported from Western powers such as France and Great Britain who had influenced the educational and legal systems of Egypt in the nineteenth century. The original title of this organization that would become the dominant social organization in Egypt and parts of the Middle East in the twentieth century was the Society of Muslim Brothers and latter known as the Muslim Brotherhood.

In many ways this organization became the social fabric of Egyptian society.

The Society clearly answered an urgent need because it would become one of the most powerful players in Egyptian politics. By the time of Banna's assassination in 1949, it had two thousand branches throughout Egypt, and the Brotherhood was the only Egyptian organization that organized every social group — civil servants, students, urban workers, and peasants. The Society was not a militant organization but sought simply to bring modern institutions to the Egyptian public in a familiar Islamic setting.[18]

When President Nasser seized power in 1952 he at first attempted to court the Muslim Brotherhood but his attempted assassination by members of a terrorist wing of the Brotherhood called the Apparatus led to government efforts to imprison many of its leaders. One of the Brothers who was imprisoned in 1954 was Sayid Qutb (1906-1966), the leading propagandist for the Brotherhood. During this period Qutb developed a dualistic theology that became the hallmark of future jihadists who followed many of the tenets in his book, *Milestones*. Qutb's program distorted Islamic history, since it made no mention of Muhammad's nonviolent policy at Hudaybiyya, the turning point of the conflict with Mecca. Humiliation, foreign occupation, and secularizing aggression had created an Islamic history of grievance. Qutb now had a paranoid vision of the past, seeing only a relentless succession of enemies — pagans, Jews, Christians, Crusaders, Mongols, Communists, capitalists, colonialists, and Zionists—intent on the destruction of Islam.[19]

In our trip through Egypt in 2010 I had the opportunity to interact with some members of the Muslim Brotherhood who had survived various attempts to suppress them by the Mubarak regime which had been in power for 30 years after the assassination of Anwar Sadat in 1981.Mubarak was still in power when we traveled throughout Egypt in 2010 but there was a massive military or police presence wherever we went. In our dialogue sessions with students they had to be very careful about what they might say since government informants were often located in the major educational institutions such as Al-Azhar University. In the year following our visit to Egypt with a large American delegation we began to see the fall of the Mubarak regime with the rise of the Arab Spring. One of the key guides for our trip to Egypt began to emerge as a leader in the Muslim Brotherhood political movement that became a strong public voice after the fall of the Mubarak regime.

The election of a new government in 2012 followed the overthrow of Hosni Mubarak in 2011.

The new leader of the Egyptian government was Mohammad Morsi, a member of the Muslim Brotherhood. He was in office for only about one year. Even though he was the first president ever elected in Egypt's long history, he attempted to impose a form of political Islam upon the country by claiming legislative and executive authority without judicial oversight. This led to massive demonstrations in June of 2013 and his removal from office by a military coup on July 3, 2013 led by General Abdul Fatah al-Sisi. Sisi took control of the government and soon emerged as the unquestioned leader of the country and began to consolidate his power by arresting and imprisoning most of the opposition to military rule, including almost all the leaders of the Muslim Brothers who remained in Egypt after the coup. This concentration of power has led to new outbreaks of terrorism particularly within the Sinai Peninsula of Egypt. The most famous incident was the downing of a Russian passenger jet with 224 tourists aboard in October of 2015. Egyptian and Russian authorities now acknowledge that a bomb was placed aboard the plane prior to its departure from the Sinai Peninsula.

Egypt has been a source for much of the ideology and jihadist theology that led to the birth of Al Qaeda. The leader of Al Qaeda today is Ayman al-Zawahiri who probably resides in Pakistan. He began his career as a medical doctor in Egypt but was also as a member of the Muslim Brotherhood. He was the personal physician for Osama bin Laden during much of the time they were in Afghanistan. Al-Zawahiri has now been surpassed in notoriety as a jihadist leader by Abu Bakr al-Baghdadi who is the leader of the Caliphate in Iraq and Syria. Recently al-Zawahiri indicated an interest in linking up Al Qaeda with jihadists operating in Southeast Asia, again indicating the global reach of his movement. The second audio speech delivered by Zawahiri is episode eight of al Qaeda's "Islamic Spring" series. It is more than 24 minutes long. Zawahiri focuses primarily on Southeast Asia, especially Indonesia, Malaysia and the Philippines. He claims that the region is ripe for a jihadist revival, just like other parts of the world.[20]

The radicalization of Egyptian youth has taken place in the context of the growth of the Muslim Brotherhood as the principal organization acting to bring together large segments of the Egyptian population under the banner of a form of political Islam. It was not originally a jihadist organization but elements of it turned in that direction out of frustration with the Egyptian government's western, secularizing tendencies. Even though the Muslim Brotherhood has been largely suppressed by the military government of General Sisi it still retains a large base of popular support in Egypt and other parts of the Middle East. The ability of jihadist groups such as Al Qaeda and ISIS to recruit members from Egypt has been enhanced by the arrest and imprisonment of many members of the Muslim Brotherhood. The marginalization of major organizations such as the Brotherhood in Egypt does not leave much room for civil society groups to become active in promoting freedom of speech and freedom of association.

Many of the human and civil rights advocacy groups are now under attack in Egypt with increasing frequency by the military regime of General Sisi. One of the groups that has represented members of the Muslim Brotherhood in government actions against it is the Arabic Network for human Rights Information founded by Hassam Baghat. This organization and its founder may soon find itself closed down and Mr. Baghat in prison like many of the individuals that he has represented through his organization.[21]

The growth of political repression in Egypt and other parts of the Middle East cannot be underestimated as a cause for the growth of political Islam and its extremist versions found within the jihadist groups that seek violent overthrow of their own governments such as we have seen occur in Egypt. The Al Qaeda network under the influence of the Egyptian medical doctor, Ayman al Zawahiri, has expressed support for the Sinai Peninsula attacks. Another link to the Muslim Brotherhood was the charismatic Palestinian scholar, Abdullah Azzam who joined the Brotherhood at age 16 while studying Shariah in Syria. Later as a student at Al Azhar University he supervised Brotherhood Youth. While he was a lecturer at Abd al-Asiz University in Jeddah, Saudi Arabia, one of his pupils was the young Bin Laden. "The life of the Muslim Ummah," Azzam declared, "is solely dependent on the ink of its scholars and the blood of its martyrs. Scholarship was essential to deepen the Ummah's spirituality, but so was the self-sacrifice of its warriors, since no nation had ever achieved distinction without a strong military. History does not write its lines except in blood."[22]

Azzam, however, did not condone the type of violent actions supported by Bin Laden and al-Zawahiri. He had a vastly different view of Jihad than that which became popularized by Al Qaeda and its offshoots. Azzam insistently maintained the orthodox view that killing noncombatants or fellow Muslims like Sadat violated fundamental Islamic teaching. In fact, he believed that a martyr could be a "witness" to divine truth even if he died peacefully in bed.[23] One of leaders of the 9/11 attacks was Mohammad Atta who flew the American Airlines plane into the World Trade Center in New York. Atta was born in Egypt and obtained a degree in architecture in 1990 from Cairo University. He then continued his studies at a Technical University in Hamburg, Germany. While in Hamburg he joined a jihadist cell that would solidify his violent ideology and prepare him for the 9/11 mission.

As moderate members fell away from the cell, they were replaced by others who shared Atta's views. In such closed groups, isolated from any divergent opinion, Sargeman believes, "the cause" becomes the milieu in which they live and breathe. Members become deeply attached to one another, shared apartments, ate and prayed together, and watched endless battlefield videos from Chechnya. Most important, they identified closely with these distant struggles. [24]

The power of groups psychology can be found in many forms but is particularly relevant to terrorist network cells that have emerged in the past two decades. Most of the time these cells are invisible to the general public so that they can exist in a variety of settings but usually within urban societies where they can plan and plot their attacks. We know that most of these cells are part of a tightly knit authority structure that bears many of the characteristics of a religious cult. Those who become part of the inner circle gain a higher level of acceptance by the charismatic leader or leaders of the cult. They gain their interior psychological balance by proving to the authorities that they are worthy not only of acceptance but also of the rewards promised by complete acquiescence to the plan set forth by the cult leader and fulfillment of their role in accomplishing the goals and objectives of the jihadist ideology. Peer pressure becomes one of the forces that keeps group members under the control of the jihadist leadership and its central council. Zimbardo explains some of the principles behind the socialization of those committed to undergo even death to gain the approval of the group's inner circle.

Peer pressure has been identified as one social force that makes people, especially adolescents, do strange things – anything — to be accepted. However, the quest for the Inner Ring is nurtured from within. There is no peer-pressure power without that push from self-pressure for them to want you. It makes people willing to suffer though painful, humiliating initiation rites in fraternities, cults, social clubs or the military.[25]

As we have already discussed, the most powerful social organization in Egypt prior to the overthrow of President Hosni Mubarak was the Muslim Brotherhood which then emerged triumphant after the 2011 Egyptian revolution. The Brotherhood represented a form of political Islam in the Middle East threatening the stability of the other autocratic regimes of the Middle East. It had emerged as a pan Arabist movement with members and an organizational structure in most of the Sunni Muslim world of the Middle East. Part of the ideology of the Brotherhood was that a political movement inspired by Islam would help to reform the countries of the Middle East and confront Israel and its allies in the US and Europe.

During his tenure as president Morsi was able to negotiate the end of the Gaza attacks by Israel in 2012 and he seemed headed to an important role in the Middle East in conjunction withTurkey which aligned itself with the Morsi administration. The coup by General Sisi not only removed Morsi but banned the Muslim Brotherhood in Egypt, seized all of its assets and put Morsi and other leaders of the Muslim Brotherhood on trial. In 2015 an Egyptian court sentenced Morsi and other leaders of the Brotherhood to a death sentence. The Brotherhood is now considered a terrorist organization in Egypt and anyone connected with it subject to criminal penalties and imprisonment. Given the long history of the Brotherhood in Egypt and the Middle East, these events can only serve to isolate their followers and turn them toward a more radical interpretation of political Islam to which some were already sympathetic. Even though there is no real evidence to date of a direct connection between the followers of the Muslim Brotherhood and ISIS or Al Qaeda, the level of violent attacks against Egypt has escalated after the coup which removed Mohammad Morsi.

> The surge in violence began in late June (2015) when Egypt's chief prosecutor was killed in a car bombing in daylight in an upscale Cairo neighborhood. Two days later, the ISIS-affiliated militants launched a massive assault on military positions in north Sinai, attempting to seize control of a small chunk of territory in Egypt. At least 17 Egyptian soldiers died, although some reports placed the death toll much higher.[26]

A power struggle has developed in the Sinai region of Egypt between followers of ISIS and Al Qaeda indicating that these groups will be seeking recruits not just in the Sinai but throughout Egyptian society which now must survive further economic hardships because of the decline in tourism. Tourism has supplied many Egyptians with employment since Egypt has one of the richest inventories of ancient historical sites from Cairo down the Nile river to Luxor. The actions of the Sisi government to repress dissent will only fuel more insurgencies and attract more recruits for Islamist groups.

The United States is focused on the military fight with ISIS and Al Qaeda but the United States fails to see how the policies of repressive governments act as a recruitment platform for the Islamist insurgency in the Middle East. As already indicated, Egypt has a growing population of about 90 million compared to 22 million in Syria and 26 million in Saudi Arabia. Egypt has also been the leading cultural and educational center of the Arab world for several centuries, which endangers both Egypt and the larger Arab world.

Students who are seeking to become scholars of Sunni Islam come to Cairo to study at Al Azhar University which was founded in the tenth century and has been the center of research and study of Islam for over a millennium. The United States State Department does bring some of these young Al Azhar scholars to the United States and I have participated in seminars with them both in Egypt and the United States. It is vital to the future of the relations between the United States and the Sunni Muslim world to expand such programs and deepen the dialogue with these young men. Most of them have had little or no contact with the world outside of Egypt. This past November a group of these scholars came to the Parliament of World Religions meeting in Salt Lake City. In my conversations with them it was clear that the idea of religious and cultural pluralism was a new idea and experience which they were trying to absorb.

The future of Egypt and the Middle East now stands at a precarious juncture. As we enter another presidential term and new United States administration, the United States needs to reevaluate its strategies for the containment of groups such as Al Qaeda and ISIS. The youth of the Middle East need to see role models who can bridge the gap between the cultures of the Middle East and western nations such as the United States and Great Britain. Internet use in the Middle East as of 2015 now exceeds 50% with over 120 million people who utilize it out of a population of about 236 million.[27] Internet access in the Middle East and North Africa, one of the major centers for jihadist recruitment and influence, will only continue to grow over the next decades as more and more youth gain access to inexpensive mobile devices such as smart phones and iPads. The struggle for access to these youths will now be concentrated over the Internet, and those who master its usage and use it will to form the meta-narrative of the future.

The youth of the world and the Middle East need to hear and believe in a vision that will build the world rather than destroy it. We have seen young people flock to the message of Bernie Sanders in the United States and organize in support of his campaign for the presidency. Over 30% of the population in the Middle East is between the ages of 15 and 29. While progress has been made in increasing the levels of literacy in many areas of the Middle East and North African, the low level of technical education still remains a major factor of concern. The Information Age in which we now live demands high levels of sophisticated technological education based on high levels of computer and software knowledge and ability to apply these skills to real world issues and problems.

"In every country in the MENA (Middle East North Africa) region, Arab youth, entrepreneurs, civil society advocates, and others are attempting to bring about positive change for both youth and their communities through innovative education initiatives. are making large investments to advance their education systems . . . Moreover, a growing number of leaders in the Arab world recognize that incremental education reform is not enough. The rapid evolution of information technology has ushered in the Information Age, creating a fundamentally different world of work than what the region has been preparing its youth for." (Castelli 20011)[28]

The further development of information technology in the Middle East and North Africa will be crucial for the integration of youth into the economies of this region. As we have seen in the United States various types of online education have mushroomed over the past two decades. Many of those taking advantage of this type of education are lower income, working adults. It is now possible to live-steam educational materials over the Internet and create interactive groups that are not limited to a specific time or place (asynchronous educational platforms). The United States and other Western nations have access to these cutting edge technologies such as versions of Skype which need to be made accessible to the youth of the Middle East and eventually all of Africa. Satellite access to the Internet will continue to grow throughout the Middle East and Africa over the next decade.

By engaging the youth of this region in the development of their technical skills we can lift their aspirations and provide a path toward greater economic and social security. We will examine some of the initiatives that are now in the embryonic stages of development.

We can take hope in the future by examining recent developments to curb carbon emissions through a global accord. Youth have played a key role in supporting the environmental movement in the Western world; now we need their participation in a dialogue with the youth of the Middle East and Africa.

In the month of April, 2016 the Paris Climate Agreement was signed by as many as 155 nations. Pope Francis has joined with a chorus of other international religious business and political leaders to embrace the steps taking place in the Paris Climate Agreement. The United States and China, which together account for nearly 40 percent of global emissions, formally signed the Paris Agreement in 2016 but President Trump removed the United States from the agreement in 2017. Despite the removal by the United States, many cities and states in the United Sates Intend to honor the accord. California governor Jerry Brown will lead a Global Climate Summit in San Francisco from September 12 to September 14, 2018 to renew its commitment and other cities and states to the Paris Accord. [29]

The Paris Climate Agreement is wonderful example of how the moral authority of religious leaders can influence the most pressing issues of our day. Pope Francis' environmental encyclical, *Laudato Si*, played a key role in building global support for the Paris climate accord. The global movement to end violence and warfare in the world is growing just as we have seen the environmental movement take hold in the public imagination spurring the political will to bring about this global agreement. A major focus of the 2016 Parliament of World Religions was the work of interfaith global spiritual leaders joining their energies to promote a peaceful, just and sustainable world social order.

Teilhard de Chardin foresaw the growth of a global ethical consciousness early at the beginning of the twentieth century. Because of his emphasis on the whole, Teilhard was a harbinger of ethical currents that are taking prominence in our time. Buzzwords are globalization, solidarity, ecology and the common good. Each of these terms makes clear – in a way that the older emphasis on divine commands, natural law, or human rights did not — that the ethical task refers to building communities, the whole human race, and the earth itself.[30]

The celebration of Earth Day on April, 2016 marked historic advances in our progress toward a more livable earth. In addition to the signing of the Paris Climate Agreement, 2016 marked a turning point, the global effort to move from a fossil fuel economy to one based upon renewable energy [31] The movement toward a new type of economy is relevant to the issues we have attempted to define in this book with regard to the growth of violent extremist groups. We can build a counter narrative for these youth that will turn them away from violence and hatred toward a new world order undergirded by social and economic structures that will give them a vital role in building the Earth. Just as the environmental movement brought together popular education, religious leadership and governmental actions on a national and global level, so also the conversion of our youth to non-violent forms of participation and social action will necessitate a broad coalition of popular movements for social and economic change in the Middle East and North Africa supported by similar groups in the Western world. Religious and moral leadership both at the grass roots and global levels needs to inform popular education in these areas of the world and partner with new forms of economic development based upon the information age in which we now live.

The seelection of Donald Trump as president of the United States can be viewed as a setback to these global solidarity movements that we have described as animating social change in the Middle East, the Paris Climate Agreement and efforts to eliminate the threat of nuclear weapons through multi-lateral agreements such as the nuclear agreement with Iran. In its annual report Human Rights Watch singled out the election of Donald Trump and the rise of populist leaders in Europe as threats to the human rights gains that have been made since the Civil Rights era of ML King.

> The election of Donald Trump as president of the United States and the rise of populist leaders in Europe poses a "profound threat" to human rights, U.S.-based Human Rights Watch warned on Thursday in its annual global report. The 687-page report reviews human rights practices in more than 90 countries. "Trump and various politicians in Europe seek power through

appeals to racism, xenophobia, misogyny and nativism," Ken Roth, executive director of Human Rights Watch, said. "The rise of populism poses a profound threat to human rights." [32]

Despite the obvious setback in the political realm in many nation states, the globalizing forces found within the structure of the Internet cannot be easily turned back. Those who master these forces will likely be the creators of the future global civilization that is presently under development throughout the world. Political leaders and political parties cannot contain the global forces that will eventually transform the xenophobic nationalism and racism have overtaken much of the developed world at this time but still represents a small minority of the world community. [33]

Reference

1   Paul Gill, "Assessing Contemporary trends and Future Prospects in the Study of the Suicide Bomber," *Negotiation & Conflict Management Research*: August 1, 2012. Retrieved from EBSCOhost, 239-240.

2   *Ibid.*, 241.

3   Philip Zimbardo, *The Lucifer Effect: Understanding How Good People Turn Evil* (Random House: New York, 2007) 219.

4   Kenan Malik, "The Little We Know About Jihadists in Our Midst," *International New York Times,* March 30, 2016.

5   *Ibid.*

6   Mia Blum, "Chasing Butterflies and Rainbows: A Critique of Kruglanski . . . Fully Committed: Suicide Bombers' Motivation and The Quest for Personal Significance"." *Political Psychology* 30.3 (2009): 387-395. *Academic Search Premier.* Web. 15 Apr. 2016. 387.

7   Victor Frankl, Love, Suffering and the Meaning of Life. Quoted in: http://www.edbatista.com/2010/04/life

8   Peter Barglow, "Understanding Radical Youth Terrorism," professional paper given at seminar on end of life in Berkeley, CA on 12/1/2015 sponsored by University of California, Berkeley.

9   *Ibid.*

10   Zimbardo, *The Lucifer Effect. 221*

11   *Blum, Op.*Cit. 388.

12   Zimbado, *Op.Cit.* 222

13 Roger Cohen, "The Islamic State of Molenbeek," *New York Times*, April 11, 2016

14 Humayun Ansari, "Islamophobia Rises in British Society," *Al Jazeera*, July 8, 2013. http://www.aljazeera.com/indepth/opi.nion/2013/07/201374135331488994.html

15 Karen Armstrong, *The Battle for God* (Ballantine: 2001)

16 Karen Armstrong, *Fields of Blood* (Alfred Knops: 2014), 316.

17 *Ibid.*, 319.

18 *Ibid.*, 320-321.

19 *Ibid.*, 322.

20 Thomas Joscelyn, "Al Qaeda Releases Three New Messages from Ayman al Zawahiri," *The Long War Journal*, January 14, 2016. http://www.longwarjournal. org/archives/2016/01/al-qaeda-releases-3-new-messages-from-ayman-al-zawahiri.php

21 Gamal Eidapril, "Egypt's Hollowed Out Society," *New York Times*, April 17, 2016.

22 Karen Armstrong, *Fields of Blood*, 368.

23 *Ibid.*, 369.

24 *Ibid.*, 382.

25 Zimbardo, 259.

26 Jared Masin, *Time*, July 23, 2015. http://time.com/3969596/egypt-isis-sinai/

27 Internet World State Usage and Population Statistic. http://www.Internetworldstats.com/stats5.htm

28 Maysa Jalbout, "Will the Technology Disruption Widen or Close the Skill Gap in the Middle East and North Africa," *Broolings*, March 25, 2016.

29 Karl Ritter and Cara Anna, "Paris Climate Agreement on Track for Early Start," ABC *News* and Associated Press, April 21, 2016. The Paris Climate Agreement went into effect on November 4, 2016. http://abcnews.go.com/US/wireStory/paris-climate-deal-track-early-start-38559897

30 Edward Vacek, SJ, "An Evolving Christian Morality," *From Teilhard to Omega: Co-Creating an Unfinished Universe* (Maryknoll, NY: Orbis, 2014) 158.

31 John D. Sutter, "Earth Day: We're not as doomed as you think," *CNN*, April 22, 2016.

32 Reuters, January 12, 2017. Trump, European Populists are a threat to human rights: Human Rights Watch. *http://www.reuters.com/article/us-humanrights-report-usa-idUSKBN14W242*

33 China's president, Xinhua, will deliver a defense of globalization at the World Economic Forum from January 17 to 20 in Switzerland. As the world's largest nation in size of population, China depends upon the use of its labor force to provide employment for its 1.35 billion people, the largest number of any nation state.

The Chinese premier will promote "inclusive" globalization at the World Economic Forum.

http://www.reuters.com/article/us-davos-meeting-china-idUSKBN14U11PF

For a vigorous defense of globalization by a world renowned economic, Jagdish Bhagwati, see his Book: *In Defense of Globalization*. (Oxford University Press: 2007).

Chapter Five

ISLAM AND THE WESTERN WORLD: PATHS TO INTEGRATION

The lack of understanding about Islam in the Western world has led to a growing fear and even paranoia about Islamic extremism and its potential to harm the Western world and Western interests in other parts of the world. The lack of Muslim extremist influences within the major Muslim religious and civic organizations in the United States can be attributed in part to the integration of the Muslim community into the fabric of American life. Most Muslims in the United States are living within the mainstream of American culture and taking advantage of American higher education and employment opportunities. According to the Pew Research Center Muslims have an employment rate quite similar to that of the rest of American population (41% have full time employment compared to 45% of the general American population). The percentage of Muslims who have graduated from college, 26%, is comparable to the general American population where 28% have graduated from college. Since the Muslim American population is mainly composed of recent immigrants the average income for Muslims is somewhat lower than that for the American public at large – 40% of American Muslims report income of $40,000 to $100,000 while 48% of the overall American population report incomes within this range. The majority of American Muslims were not born in the United States yet they pose no threat to the United States. Over 60% of Muslims in the United States are either first or second generation immigrants to the United States. Only 37% were born in the United States.

The picture that emerges of American Muslims according to the Pew Research Report on American Muslims is that they generally mirror the experience of other immigrant groups that have come to the United States over the past two centuries.[1] The level of their participation in American life indicates that American Muslims who now number about 3.1 million will continue their growth over the next decade since they have a higher birth rate than the general American population. The Muslim population, according to the most recent report of the Pew Center, will more than double to about 8 million by 2050 and become the second largest religious group after those who identify as Christians.[2] The proportion of Muslims in the United States will eventually mirror their proportion found in the world at large by the middle of the twenty-first century. The United States can now serve as a laboratory for the interfaith relationship of Muslims and Christians. Muslims in the United States are not more isolated or more marginalized than other immigrant groups that have come to the United States over the past centuries.

At a recent talk given at Santa Clara University 9 (May 18, 2016), Sheik Hamza Yusuf, President of Zaytuna College in Berkeley, CA, the first Muslim liberal arts college in the United States, stated that the Muslim experience in the United States has been largely favorable and cannot be compared with the discrimination experienced by the African Americans, Native Americans, Japanese Americans and Chinese Americans over the course of American history. Sheik Yusuf is considered one of the key contributors to the Marrakesh Declaration already mentioned in a previous chapter.

The stereotype of Muslims that we find in the American media does not fit the actual lives that they lead here in the United States. Stereotypes are constructions of the imagination based upon our unconscious projection of states of fear that are very powerful in the United States culture and became part of the 2016 presidential debate. As a gun-oriented culture we perceive the "Other" as the enemy with whom we are in a struggle for survival. So much of our popular culture, particularly action films, is based upon this unconscious projection of the Other as enemy but which really is living inside us; a mental dystopia. Every time a terrorist incident occurs in some part of the world, it only reinforces the level of paranoia which exists in the Western world toward those who practice the Muslim faith.

We know rationally that we are much more in danger of death whenever we drive a car than becoming a victim of a terrorist incident. Over 50,000 Americans die ear year of car accidents yet we do not experience the same level of perceived threat from driving a car as we do in reading about a terrorist act. In order to overcome this irrational fear of Islam and the Muslim faith, we need to take time to understand the origins of the Islamic faith and its historical development over the past 1400 years. The religion of Islam took hold in the tribal culture of what is today Saudi Arabia. Much of the early history of Islam was dominated by three Caliphates, the first is known as the Rashidun Caliphate led by the first four successors to the Prophet Mohammad. These are the four men who led the first Caliphate: Abu Bakr (632-634 CE), Umar (634-644 CE), Uthman (644-656 CE), and Ali, (656-661 CE.)

The sectarian split in Islam between The Shia and Sunni denominations of Islam occurred over the death of Ali and the election of a new Caliph who was not a hereditary successor to the Prophet Mohammad.

For Muslims the Caliph was both a spiritual and political leader for the entire Muslim *Umma* (community) within the context of the tribal era. There was no secular state at this time in the Arabian Peninsula and even today, in some parts of the Middle East and North Arica, tribal cultures still exist among the Bedouins. The Prophet Mohammad was aware of the Christian empire of the Byzantines which controlled two of the major cities of the Middle East, Damascus and Jerusalem. The Jewish community was well represented in Medina, the place where the Muslim *Umma* first appeared in 622 CE, when the Prophet Mohammad emigrated (*hijra*) from Mecca to Medina with his original followers. This date is considered year one in the Muslim lunar calendar.

The Constitution of Medina was the first written document in the ancient world giving rights of citizenship and religious freedom to the Jewish community in Medina as well all of the 12 tribal groups that existed there. The Muslim scholars who recently met in Morocco affirmed that this document should be the basis for freedom of religion among religious minorities in Muslim majority countries. It also counters the claim that Muslims wish to impose their faith upon non-Muslim populations when they gain power. After the death of Mohammad in 632 CE, the question arose about whether the new monotheistic religion of Islam would continue or would it end with the death of the Prophet. The first Caliph following the Prophet Mohammad stated that the new order established by the revelation of the Qur'an and the life of the Prophet was now the new order for the entire region under its control.

Quoting the Qur'an 3:144:

> Muhammad is only a messenger and many (other) messengers have gone before him.
> So if he dies or is killed, would you turn back on your heels (to unbelief)?
> He who turns back on his heels will do no harm to Allah at all,
> But Allah will reward the faithful.

Some of the Arab tribes claimed that their agreement with the Prophet ended upon his death. But Abu Bakr declared that their agreement was not with the man, Mohammad, but rather with Allah. "Abu Bakr's campaign constitutes an important precedent, pointing to a special relationship between religion and politics. – in Arabic, between *Al-ridda* (religion, law, custom, that to which one Is obligated, and which connects one to another) and *al-dunya* (the affairs of the world, including economics, ordinary political activity, and the life."[4]

By the time of the death of Umar, the second Caliph in the growing Muslim empire, Muslim miltary forces controlled Egypt, Syro-Palestine and most of Iraq. Under the next two Caliphs, Uthman and Ali, the empire expanded to include the remainder of Iraq and much of Iran.

Within the Islamic faith the clear connection was now implanted between the sphere of religious faith and the social and political realm in which that faith existed. According to Muslim belief, there was no separation between the interior spiritual life of the believer and the outward realm of the society in which he or she lived along with the laws *(Sharia)* which governed that society.

The Umayyad Caliphate based in Damascus (661-750 CE) did succeed the first four Caliphs and witnessed the beginning of conflict between Sunni and Shia denominations of the Islamic faith. The Umayyad Caliphate advanced the Islamic culture throughout the Maghreb (western North Africa) and much of the Iberian Peninsula. The period of the Umayyad Caliphate resulted in the expansion of the Islamic empire into the largest ever known up to that point in human history. The Caliph ruled this empire through a number of provincial governors who would report to him. This period also reflected some challenges to the authority of the Umayyad Caliphate. The question of who actually speaks for the Islamic faith still remains a question in Islam today. At times in Islamic history the Caliph has been the principal spokesperson for the Ummah but in more recent history the group of leading Islamic religious scholars has claimed to be the final authority in matters of interpretation of the faith based upon the study of the Qur'an, Hadith and the life of the Prophet *(Sunnah)*.

Confusion arose once the Islamic tradition split into two rival camps: the Sunni tradition which represents the great majority of Muslims and the Shia which is now represented largely by a Shia population located principally in Iran and Iraq. Since there was no separation of the political realm and the realm of faith within the early Islamic tradition, the rulers of Muslim majority states today often claimed authority over the spiritual and political realms with Saudi Arabia (Sunni) and Iran (Shia) as two of the prime examples. The Abbasid Caliphate (750-1258 CE) represented the "Golden Age" of Islamic culture when Islam influenced the development of a highly intellectual culture in Baghdad. It developed in conjunction with Jewish and Christian scholars who were familiar with Greek philosophy, science and political thought. The Abbasid Caliphs set up an institute in Baghdad which was known as the House of Wisdom (*Bayt al Hikma*). This institute specialized in translating Greek scientific and philosophical texts into Arabic and also systematized and organized the natural sciences and the applied sciences such as medicine and astronomy.

Some theologians who claim to be associated with the kind of dialectical theology Muslims called *al-kalam*, literally "speech", in this context 'theological disputation.' The latter view held that the import of the Qur'an was best extracted through a process of rigorous, systematic argument. The most influential of these, in the early years of Abbasid rule, came to be known as Mu'tazilites, separatists. Mutazilites focused on clarifying the system of doctrine outlined in the Qur'an.[5]

The relationship of faith to reason became one of the dominant issues in medieval Islam and Christianity. The role of philosophical and theological argumentation became part of the core of both Muslim and Christian scholarly debate. An example of this type of debate was the argumentation that took place between Al Ghazali and Ibn Rushd (Averroes) on the role of philosophy in its applicability to religious revelation. This theme has become part of the dialogue between Christianity and Islam in the contemporary era. Pope Benedict XVI brought up this matter in his famous 2006 Regensburg lecture which aroused much contention within the Islamic world. His lecture seemed to infer that the justification for violent jihad within Islamic theology resulted from the lack of balance between faith and reason within the Islamic canon. It is clear that in the history of Islam there have been long periods in which philosophy and science were not only well represented but which were a dominant motif in Islamic culture. This was particularly the case during the period of the Abassid Caliphate which lasted for five centuries from about 750 CE to 1250 CE when Baghdad was the intellectual center of the Arab world and empire.

When the Mongols attacked Baghdad and destroyed their libraries and killed their leaders and scholars, this period of history came to a violent end. This traumatic event led to an attempt to return to the sources of Islamic piety in the Qur'an and Haidith with more of an emphasis upon Islamic law (*Sharia*) and normative interpretation. The decline of critical thinking and philosophical reasoning within the training of Muslim religious leaders continued well into the modern era which opened the door for various types of religious fundamentalist currents of thought including those that justified an interpretation of Islamic theological sources such as not allowing *ijtihad* or the use of independent reasoning in the interpretation of the Qur'an or other theological sources.

In effect the role of theology was limited to stating "proof" texts about established positions in the canon of Islamic theology. At his recent talk given at Santa Clara University, Sheik Humza Yusuf emphasized the need for the skills of argumentation taught in the medieval trivium of grammar, rhetoric and logic. The reasoning skills which were part of the medieval paradigm of education are necessary today to combat the fundamentalist thinking found in groups such as Al Qaeda and ISIS. Muslim and Christian religious teachers can benefit by studying the classical liberal arts to fully learn how to examine the variety of ways to interpret Sacred Scriptures such as the Bible and the Qur'an. Hans Kung characterizes the problems facing religious scholars following the collapse of the Abbasid Caliphate and the rise of the Ottoman empire.

> The new rulers, often uncultivated and barely educated, were dependent on the old elites particularly in training their cadres. The Ulama (religious leaders), most of whom were both theological and legal scholars, gradually became responsible for higher education. They formed law schools, with well-organized bodies of teachers and pupils. They took pains to train judges, notaries, legal experts and justiciaries. Alongside the law schools were special schools of theologians, which, though they had no judicial and administrative functions, acquired a coherent social identity, much like the Mu'taziilah and the Ash'arite schools. [6]

These groups or religious scholars began to assume an ever more important role in becoming the authoritative source for interpretation of scriptural texts and the teachings of the Prophet. In the era following the

Abbasid Caliphate the madrasah or seminary became the customary way for someone to attain standing as a religious leader within Sunni Islam. The concept of "Islamic sciences" began to be the core understanding of what could be taught within the curriculum of the madrasahs. These included study of the text of the Qur'an, the Hadiths and one of the schools of Islamic law called Sharia.

The understanding of "science" or the philosophy of nature as understood by Aristotle became quite different in Western culture after the period of the Abbasid Caliphate had ended.

Aristotelian philosophy was not generally taught as part of the curriculum in the madrasah because it was viewed as not conforming to revelation found in the Qur'an and the life and teachings of the Prophet and his early followers (Sunnah). The idea of independent schools of natural science did not exist within the curriculum of the madrasah. The role of Islamic law or Shariah grew in importance during this period and became the normative governing influence in the lives of those living in Muslim majority countries.

> The Shariah formed the uniting center of Sunni Islam. But some Muslims asked (and still ask) don't all the legal scholars and all the legal learning express only quite particular aspects of Islam and neglect others? Indeed, and it would become increasingly clear that the existing religious needs of individuals and later the broad population of Shariah Islam could not really be satisfied just by the formulation of laws and their imposition as the will of Allah.[7]

The growth of a popular spirituality within Sunni Islam known as Sufism became the dominant religious movement in Muslim majority countries during the later medieval era (tenth to fourteenth centuries).

> The original Sufis were not mystics in the real sense, proclaiming a doctrine and experience of unity, but rather ascetics, including many who despised and

provoked existing society and were even active fighters for the glory of the faith (Jihad) in the Muslim frontier settlements.. . . Sufism accepts asceticism (*zuhd*) but also transcends it as one of the "stations" on the 'way'. Turning Inward and striving for immediate unity with God is characteristic of the Sufis in the classical sense.[8]

Similar to Catholicism, which venerated the graves of saints, Sufi holy men were highly respected in many parts of the Muslim majority areas of North Africa, the Middle East and South Asia. In the contemporary era the Sufi shrines have been under attack by fundamentalist groups within Islam. In 2012 during the Benghazi attack on the US Consulate, Sufi Shrines in three Libyan cities were destroyed. Perhaps we don't hear much about these incidents because attacks on Sufis and Sufi sites have become routine, not just in Libya, but throughout the Islamic world. This past summer, Islamic militants in Mali demolished historical mausoleums, universities and libraries in the ancient Saharan trading town of Timbuktu, several of which were on UNESCO's list of world heritage sites.[9]

We have seen that Islamic law or Sharia grew in importance within Islam during the Abbasid Caliphate and took on the form of an Islamic orthodoxy, particularly within the Hanbali school of Islamic jurisprudence. Ahmed ibn Hanbali (d. 855 CE) promoted a more literal interpretation of the Qur'an, Hadith and the testimony of his early followers. This school of jurisprudence and the theology underlying it became the forerunner of the Wahhabi and Salafist movements in Saudi Arabia and Egypt. Similar to the orthodoxy of the medieval Catholic church which resulted in the persecution of heretics, the Hanbali form of Sharia allows a variety of corporal punishments for those who are guilty of disobeying its statutes. Criminal law punishments in Saudi Arabia include public beheading, hanging, stoning, amputation and lashing. Many of the punishments used by ISIS can also be found codified in the Hanbali legal code which is still operative in Saudi Arabia and some other states in the Middle East. The key Islamic

Sharia theorist used to justify extremist views of Jihad and attacks upon Christians and Muslims is Sheik Taqi ibn Tamiya (1263-1328).

> The most important fatwa upon which ISIS bases its holy war or jihad is the "Mardin" fatwa . . . ., Ibn Taymiyyah issued a fatwa (in 1263) encouraging the fight against Mardin and its people (although the fatwa has been a source of disagreement among Muslim scholars for a long time). Many hard-liners and advocates of the Salafist jihadi ideology perceive this fatwa as a permission to wage war, to impose Sharia even within Islamic countries[10]

The use of Islamic jurisprudence to justify extremist ideologies and violent attacks against western influences as well as other Muslim who do not accept the justification for these texts has become part of the background for how groups such as Al Qaeda and ISIS manipulate the history of Islam to promote and validate their ideology. Most of the youth who join these groups have no knowledge of the historical sources that these extremist groups use as "proof" texts showing that their behavior fits into an acceptable Islamic paradigm. Extremists can also point to certain texts of the Qur'an which seem to justify violence against non-believers. Among the most often cited verses is this one: "Kill the idolaters wherever you find them, and capture them, and blockade them, and watch for them at every lookout . . ." (Quran 9:5). The historical context of this passage seems to refer to the Meccan opponents of the Prophet Mohammad who had declared war against him and his followers. Islam is clearly not a pacifist religion but it does not condone wanton violence as we find practiced by Al Qaeda and ISIS.

The key term which can have multiple interpretation is Islam is *jihad*. Hans Kung attempts to clarify the meaning of this term which is often translated in western media as 'holy war'.

The Arabic word *jihad* does not mean precisely the same as the two English words 'holy war'; it covers a broad semantic field. Initially, it means simply 'effort', and in some passages of the Qur'an is understood as 'striving hard' on the way of God: 'And strive hard in God's cause with all the striving that is due to Him it is He who has elected you.' The combination of 'holy' and 'war' does not occur in the Qur'an; in the Islamic view, war can never be 'holy'.[11]

It is clear that after the end of the Abbasid Caliphate the practice of jihad took on a different meaning and context. The Ottoman empire began to use the teaching of jihad to justify their wars of conquest in the Balkans. With the spread of the Islamic faith to many parts of the world and with diverse constituencies including those outside the traditional center of the Islamic world in the Middle East, the practice of *jihad* became subservient to the political goals of the region of the world where Islam became a majority religion. The present day use of the term by extremist groups is an attempt to rationalize violence by returning to the medieval era in which jihad did have the connotation of an armed struggle but not a 'holy war'.

The use of a theology of jihad by fundamentalist groups does raise the question of how much the historical/critical interpretation of Islamic sources had permeated into the centers of Islamic learning. One of the key questions that arose during the Caliphate of Abd AllahAl-Ma 'mum (reigned as Caliph 813-833 CE) was the origin of the Qur'an: was it created or uncreated? Al-Ma 'mum claimed that it was created which would allow room for human interpretation of the Quran by religious scholars who would need approval by the Caliph. Those who supported this positions were called Mu'tazilites because they stress the role of reason in the interpretation of the Qur'an. The main opponent to this view was Ahmad Ibn Hanbal, the founder of the Hanbali school of Islamic jurisprudence which was previously discussed as formative of Islamic jurisprudence within Wahhabi Sunni Islam. Mu'tazili theology was heavily influenced by Greek philosophy, particularly that of Aristotle. Al Ma 'mum also is credited with establishing the House of Wisdom (*Bayt al Hikma*) during his reign which translated many Greek manuscripts into Arabic and provided an impetus for the growth of Arabic science during his reign.

The hermeneutical issue he raised about the Qur'an is still with us today. If there is only a literal sense in which the Qur'an can be read, then the passages which seem to condone violence toward non-believers and those who decide to change their religious belief could have no alternative meaning. An uncreated Qur'an seems to imply that the teachings of the Qur'an are immutable for they are co-eternal with Allah and not based on any human interpretation. Christianity has gone through a similar challenge when biblical scholars started to apply the historical approach to biblical studies. Just as the Bible must be seen in its historical context so too must the Qur'an. The statements and values exhibited in the Qur'an about jihad may allow for a new interpretation given a new set of historical conditions. One of the most influential Muslim legal scholars living in the United States, Doctor Khaled Abou El Fadl, provides a historical perspective on the question of how to interpret the Islamic heritage, both past and present. He points out that there is a split within the Islamic culture that finds two competing paradigms for the meaning of the Islamic faith in the twenty-first century. Many Muslim scholars view Islam as a peaceful religious tradition when taken in the context of its complex and diverse history.[12]

Despite this rich doctrinal and historical background, the dilemmas of a modern Muslim intellectual persist. For one, this tolerant and humanitarian Islamic tradition exists in tension with other doctrines in the Islamic tradition that are less tolerant or humanitarian. Many classical Muslim scholars, for instance, insisted on a conception of the world that is bifurcated and dichotomous. Those scholars argued that the world is divided into the abode of Islam (*dar al-Islam*) and abode of war (*dar al-harb*); the two can stop fighting for a while, but one must inevitably prevail over the other. According to these scholars, Muslims must give non-Muslims one of three options; either become Muslim, pay a poll tax, or fight.

The "clash" of civilizations may not be between Islam and Western civilization but rather a clash within Islam itself as understood by diverse religious scholars. The medieval positions about Islamic orthodoxy expressed in the Hanbali legal tradition and still predominant in some Muslim majority countries through Wahhabism runs contrary to the Enlightenment values that helped to form western democracies. One of the most well-known scholars of Islam in the United States, Dr. John Esposito, discusses the question of whether the Wahhabi version of Islam is conducive to violence and terrorism.

> Is the Wahhabi/Salafi message necessarily violent and terrorist? True, Wahhabi refers to an ultraconservative, puritanical, absolutist theology based on an uncompromising, polarized view of the world. It pits good against evil, believers against nonbelievers, and Sunni against Shia . . . . Wahhabi/Salafi interpretations remain strong but not predominant in many Muslim communities. Their exclusivist, isolationist and often intolerant theologies are no more dangerous than fundamentalisms in other faiths, but their followers will surely be ill equipped to respond to the need for religious pluralism in an increasingly globalized world, a world where millions of Muslims live in non-Muslim— majority countries.[13]

An example of the influence of religious pluralism in the United States is the city of Hamtramck, Michigan. This city is located within the city limits of Detroit and happens to be a traditionally Polish American enclave where I spent many of my childhood years.

In the past few decades the city has become home to many Muslim immigrants and now is the first city in the United States to have a Muslim majority city council. Many of the elderly Polish Americans who still live in the city are anxious about the influx of Muslim immigrants from Bangladesh, Yemen and Bosnia. Because of the high poverty rate in the city and the surrounding area of Detroit, the cost of housing is very reasonable and attractive to the Muslim immigrants where they have a strong community presence with their own mosques, ethnic grocery stories and now a strong political influence over the city government.

> Hamtramck's exceedingly low home prices and relatively low crime rate have proved especially attractive to new immigrants; whose presence is visible everywhere. Most of the women strolling Joseph Campeau Avenue wear hijabs, or headscarves, and *niqabs*, veils that leave only the area around the eyes open. Many of the markets advertise their wares in Arabic or Bengali, and some display signs telling customers that owners will return shortly — gone to pray, much in the same way Polish businesses signaled that employees had gone to Mass. [14]

The continued assimilation of the American Muslim population including Muslim immigrants from the Middle East can be a deterrent to the radicalization of Muslim youth. It will show that the United States is not an enemy to those who practice the Muslim faith and it will also help to defuse the existing tensions between the US and the Middle East. The leadership on this issue can come from the interfaith alliances that are now growing in most urban areas of the United States where Muslims now reside. In the area of the United States where I reside the diocese of San Jose is part of an interfaith organization, the Silicon Valley Interreligious Council (SVIC) which sponsors a variety of interfaith activities with the local Muslim population. Recently, the Bishop of the San Jose diocese, Reverend Patrick McGrath, hosted a luncheon for Muslim religious leaders in the City of Palo Alto at Thomas More parish. A picture of Bishop McGrath appeared prominently on the front page of the diocesan newspaper, *The Valley Catholic*.[15] These kinds of confidence- building actions can only bring Muslims and Christians in the U.S. into a mutually beneficial relationship and encourage greater cooperation and collaboration. Given the global reach of San Jose and Silicon Valley, the efforts made by the interfaith community can only help to bridge the divide that has often existed between Christianity and Islam historically.

Pope Francis has set a new tone for Christian/Muslim relations which resulted in a visit of the Grand Imam Sheik Ahmed al-Tayyib of Al Azhar Mosque which is connected to Al AzharUniversity in Cairo, the seat of Sunni Muslim learning and scholarship. Sheik Tayyib met with Pope Francis at the Vatican on May 23, 2016. It was the the first meeting of Pope Francis with the highest ranking Sunni religious leaders since the start of his pontificate, one of the actions by Pope Francis which opened the door to such a meeting after relations between the Vatican and Al Azhar had been suspended five years earlier to protest remarks by Pope Benedict about attacks on Christians in Egypt. Pope Francis has made a particular effort to reach out to Muslim immigrants who have fled from Syria in the hope of coming to Europe. Pope Francis has urged Europe and other western nations to assist in the relocation and resettlement of Syrian refugees.

> Francis and el-Tayyib spoke privately for 25 minutes in the pope's private library, bidding each other farewell with an embrace. El-Tayyib and his delegation then had talks with the Vatican cardinal in charge of interreligious dialogue. The Vatican said the meeting held a "great significance" for Catholic-Muslim dialogue. In a statement, spokesman the Rev. Federico Lombardi said Francis and el-Tayyib discussed the need for "authorities and the faithful of the world's great religions to show a common commitment to peace in the world.[15]

They also discussed the rejection of violence and extremism, and the plight of Christians "in the context of conflicts and tensions in the Mideast and their protection," the statement said.

Pope Francis has continued to explore new ways to communicate a positive message of peace and reconciliation of Christians and Muslims in which these religious bodies contribute to the ongoing dialogue of all humanity seeking world peace and understanding. Pope Francis' comments on the status of interfaith dialogue provide a foundation for institutions and organizations dedicated to the constructive engagement of Christians and Muslims in diverse parts of the world. The recent conflicts in Europe and the United States over immigration issues is one of the important areas for Christian and Muslims to take up in universities, interfaith conferences and civic events.

> He continued, "Islamic-Christian dialogue, in a special way, requires patience and humility accompanied by detailed study, as approximation and improvisation can be counterproductive and or even the cause of unease and embarrassment. There is a need for lasting and continuous commitment in order to ensure we do not find ourselves unprepared in various situations and in different contexts. Culture and education are not secondary to a true process of moving towards each other that respects in every person "his life, his physical integrity, his dignity and the rights deriving from that dignity, his reputation, his property, his ethnic and cultural identity, his ideas and his political choices.[16]"

Reference

2   Pew Research Center Report, "A new estimate of the US Muslim population," January 6, 2016.
    http://www.pew research.org/fact-tank/2016/01/06/a-new-estimate-of-the-u-s-muslim-population/
3   See Sheik Hamza "Islam, Citizenship and Religious Liberty," May 18, 2016.
    https://santaclarauniversity.hosted.panopto.com/Panopto/Pages/Viewer.aspx?id=ee572d07-2ca8-401e-a8dc-1f2b370cc85b
4   John Kelsey, *Arguing the Just War in Islam* (Cambridge, Massachusetts: Harvard University Press, 2007) 36.
5   Hans Kung, *Islam: Past, Present and Future* (Oxford: Oneworld Publications, 2007) 317
6   *Ibid,* 317
7   *Ibid.,* 322
8   *Ibid.* 325

9   Shukur Khilkhal, "ISIS emerges from radical Islamic jurisprudence," *AlMonitor*: The Pulse of the Middle East, August 12, 2014 http://www.al-monitor.com/pulse/en/originals/2014/08/religious-origins-of-islamic-extremism.html

10   Kung, *Op.Cit.*, 597.

11   Kung, *Op.Cit.*, 598.

12   Khaled Abou El Fadl, *Published in "Taking Back Islam: American Muslims Reclaim Their Faith", edited by Michael Wolfe and the producers of Beliefnet, Rodale Press, 2002.

http://www.scholarofthehouse.org/pjifrbotabai.html

13   John L. Esposito, *The Future of Islam* (Oxford: Oxford University Press, 2010) 76-77

14   Sarah Pulliam Bailey, "In the first Muslim-majority US city, residents tense about its future", *Washington Post*, November 21, 2015.

https://www.washingtonpost.com/national/for-the-first-majority-muslim-us-city-residents-tense-about-its-future/2015/11/21/45d0ea96-8a24-11e5-be39-0034bb576eee_story.html

14   "Diocese of San Jose Hosts Interfaith Luncheon with Local Muslim Community.", *The Valley Catholic*, May 10, 2016.

15   Nicole Winfield, "Pope Embraces Al-Azhar Imam in Sign of Renewed Relations", Associated Press, May 23, 2016. http://abcnews.go.com/Health/wireStory/pope-meets-al-azhar-imam-sign-renewed-relations-39301625

16   Pope Francis, January 24, 2015. Address at a meeting of the Pontifical Institute for Arabic and Islamic studies. http://www.dimmid.org/index.asp?Type=B_BASIC&SEC=%7BB56CE535-6DC7-41DA-AA53-AF4C926E2CA5%7D

Chapter Six

CONVERGENCE OF CONSCIOUSNESS THROUGH TECHNOLOGICAL INNOVATION

We have seen the role that technology played in the birth of the Arab Spring in 2010 and 2011 but its wider implication for the involvement of the youth of the Middle East and North Africa has yet to be fully articulated as part of a broader youth movement in the developed and developing areas of the world. Teilhard de Chardin predicted in the first half of the twentieth century that technological innovations would spur the convergence of humanity toward a unification of consciousness. The birth of the Internet in the latter half of the twentieth century has made possible the interaction of peoples and cultures that was not thought possible just fifty years ago prior to the Internet, the development of the personal computer, the World Wide Web and the software needed to navigate the web. The recent advances in cell phone technology have made it possible to have almost complete access to the Internet with hand-held devices such as a smartphone or tablet. The cost of these technological innovations have continued to drop over the past decade so that they have become more accessible to young people in the Middle East, North Africa and other parts of the developing world. Even though fundamentalist groups such as ISIS and Al Qaeda represent a pre-modern understanding of Islam they are adept at using the latest forms of technology such as YouTube and Twitter to promote their message to Muslim youth. The use of technology by these fundamentalist groups has tended to divide humanity and create various forms of paranoia about their attempts to infiltrate their presence into Europe and the United States. It has led to a counter movement to attack their message using the Internet as a platform for curtailing their propaganda. The western media has failed to highlight the positive developments taking place in the context of the Internet that are helping to unite rather than divide the future leaders of Europe, the United States and the Middle East and North Africa.

Teilhard de Chardin claimed that the growth of technology would lead also to a growth in consciousness that was spiritual in nature. He felt that the facts of biological evolution were not separate from the evolution of consciousness expressed through the human exchanges that led to the formation of human cultures and civilizations. This evolution, which began with earlier tribal cultures and was expressed through accompanying religious and political structures, had now advanced in the modern age to a new form of global consciousness which was transforming all previous forms of human organization such as the tribe, the nation state, and empires. For Teilhard, the age of nations was already past and the challenge before us was to build the earth drawing forth all the goodness and beauty of each human culture into a global civilization.

Teilhard's vision presumed the growth of a universal consciousness which he called the "Noosphere," a communal consciousness which transcended the thought of any individuals but which contained an underlying teleology drawing humankind toward a central focus which he called the Omega point. Teilhard believed that the Omega had to be rooted in the evolutionary Christ as the ultimate destiny of the human race. Even though Muslims and other non-Christians would dispute the identity of Omega as Christ, Muslims and non-Christians could agree that humanity must have a common destiny. All of the recent studies into the human genome have indicated that we are essentially one human species united with the capacity to form a global civilization. This globalizing force is not diminishing but growing stronger each decade that passes. For Teilhard individuation and convergence of consciousness are not incompatible but, rather, complementary.

Men cease to be self-contained individuals and join in a common cause. In them, thenceforth, the spiritual energy of the element is finally ready to integrate itself in the total energy of the Noosphere. But we must not fail to bring out an important point; the perfection and usefulness of each nucleus of human energy is in relation to the whole depend in the last resort upon whatever is unique in each of them. The great point to which the technician of the Spirit should direct his attention in dealing with human beings is to leave them the possibility of discovering themselves in the transformation which he is seeking to bring about in them and the freedom to differentiate themselves ever more and more.[1]

The idea that "union differentiates" is at the heart of Teilhard's evolutionary vision of the destiny of humanity and the whole universe. Just as the union of material forces in evolution has produced increasingly complex forms of life, so also will humanity continue to produce new and complex forms of civilization which are distinct from previous cultural forms yet provide even more intense and variegated forms of consciousness. The growth and unification of intelligent life at the biological level has a corresponding trajectory at the levels of culture and civilization. The idea of the clash of civilizations put forth by Samuel Huntington should be replaced by the evolution of western civilization away from a position of dominance to one of partnership with the diversity found in the human community of the rest of the world. By focusing our moral and intellectual energy on the regions of the world experiencing conflict, intolerance and violence, we may be able to turn the tide of human consciousness toward a world that is whole and unified. The revolutionary role of mass communications in making this possible cannot be underestimated. Teilhard foresaw the key role that computers would play in the process of human evolution.

Here I am thinking of those electronic machines (the starting point and hope of the young science of cybernetics) by which our mental capacity to calculate and combine is reinforced and multiplied by a process and degree that herald as astonishing advances in this direction as those that the optical sciences (have) already produced for our vision.[2]

The prominence of the Internet and social media in the Arab Spring are symbolic of the power of the Internet to unite individuals across traditional barriers to form mass movements that bring about social change in a very rapid fashion. Wael Ghonim was a computer engineer working for Google in the Middle East in 2011 when he established a Facebook page, "We are all Khaled Said."

This page which illustrated the brutality of the Egyptian police created a response from thousands of Egyptian youth and led to mass demonstrations in Tahrir Square which were televised around the world in 2011 and led to the the resignation of President Hosni Mubarak.[3]

The Egyptian revolution was also significant because it was a movement that mobilized millions of Egyptians across the traditional divides of religion, politics, gender and social class. Even though the revolution did not endure it still brought about a fundamental change of consciousness among the Egyptian people that will eventually lead to a new society. Millions of young people came out of the shadows of Egyptian society to participate in the revolution of 2011 which far exceeds the number of those who have turned to violent jihadist groups after the curtailment of the revolution by the Egyptian military. The use of force and violence to replace democratic methods of change cannot prevail in the long run of history. It may hold back social change for a period of time but it is not the force that bends the arc of history in the Middle East, North Africa, and the world. The Egyptian people share a common history that includes a long history of acceptance of religious pluralism for Muslims and Christians. Egypt is one of the few countries of the Middle East with a significant Christian minority population that has remained largely intact over the centuries. The myth exploited by jihadists is that Christians are part of the Crusaders invading Muslim lands. Egyptian Christians have lived in Egypt for centuries before the birth of the Muslim community.

Despite the setbacks that have occurred since 2013, the Egyptian people continue to have an increasingly literate and articulate youth population. For youth between the ages of 15 and 24 the literacy rate now exceeds 90% and the Internet usage in Egypt is now over 40 million.[4] If we can assume that universal moral principles will ultimately overcome those political systems that rely primarily on fear, force or violence to impose their will, we can see a way forward for those areas of the world now controlled either by authoritarian regimes or those under the duress of violent insurgencies. Teilhard de Chardin connected the biological, cultural and spiritual evolution of humanity in his understanding of human nature and human development.

> For us who see the development of consciousness as *the* essential phenomenon of nature, things appear in a very different light. If indeed as we have assumed the world culminates in a thinking reality, the organization of personal human energies represents the supreme stage of cosmic evolution on earth and morality is consequently nothing less than the higher development of mechanics and biology. The world is ultimately constructed by moral forces; and reciprocally, the function of morality is to construct the world [5]

Teilhard's vision of morality as an organic and emergent property of Humanity helps us to put the present crisis in a broader context. Karen Armstrong has brought out that the key development in the ancient world, centered in the Axial Age, was essentially a consciousness revolution led in great part by a shift toward higher moral reasoning. This evolution in ethical intelligence became a foundation for the rise of significant spiritual forces in diverse areas of the globe. The Axial Age was more concerned with the ethical life of humanity than with belief in certain doctrines.

The Axial Age changed this; they still valued ritual, but gave it a new ethical significance and put morality at the heart of the spiritual life. They only way you could encounter what they called "God," "Nirvana," "Brahman," or the "Way" was to live a compassionate life. Indeed, religion was compassion.[6]

Karen Armstrong is one of the key leaders in the dialogue between Christianity and Islam as well as one of the founders of the Dialogue of Civilizations. She also is the founder of the Charter for Compassion that she initiated in 2009 in conjunction with the TED prize, which she had won the previous year. This movement has largely spread through her global influence and that of other major religious leaders such as the Dalai Lama. It is clear, however, that this movement could not exist without the Internet. The Charter for Compassion has now united many other organizations around the world to support the transformation of the world on the local, national and global levels.

We believe that a compassionate world is a peaceful world. We believe that a compassionate world is possible when every man, woman, and child treats others as they wish to be treated—with dignity, equity, and respect.

We believe that all human beings are born with the capacity for compassion and that it must be cultivated for human beings to survive and thrive. *Join to make compassion a clear, luminous and dynamic force in our polarized world. Embrace the compassion revolution.*[7]

Compassion is one of the key antidotes to hatred and violence which still permeate much of the world. Educational systems throughout the world and particularly in the Middle East can find resources in the peace movement to educate the next generation. By utilizing the resources of the Internet it is possible to spread this message to much of the developing and developed world. Connecting the Middle East to Europe, and the United States has been one of the projects of Soliya Connect in which I have served as an instructor/facilitator for students located where I teach in San Jose, California. Soliya Connect is another project of the United Nations Dialogue of Civilizations. It utilizes its own interactive Internet platform to bring together students from the Middle East, Europe, and the United States in a virtual classroom setting. The program can be integrated into a college classroom setting as an online component that takes place over a period of eight weeks in which students devise a critical thinking project focused in part on the media portrayal of the Middle East.[8]

This program began in 2003 and has now spread to over 100 colleges and universities in the USA and links students together from 27 countries including many from the Middle East and North Africa. In additional to teaching students critical thinking skills about the media and Islam, the program also helps to establish relationships among the students who take the course from around the world. Many American students who cannot afford a semester abroad during their college years can gain access to a similar experience via the Internet where they have live interaction with students from the Middle East and Europe through this program. Very few of the students at San Jose City College where I teach will have funds to do a semester abroad but they can take part in the Soliya experience via a form of Skype in a critical thinking course. The Soliya program is only one example of how the creative use of the the Internet can unite youth from diverse areas of the world where misunderstanding and conflict have been predominant since 9/11. This spring I plant to utilize Skype to connect my students with other students and faculty in the Middle East and Africa.

There are numerous other examples of intercultural and interfaith programs that could be developed utilizing social media platforms. Colleges and universities need to be more adept at including these access points for dialogue programs with students from Muslim majority countries to bridge the gaps that exist between religions and cultures. The lack of employment opportunities for youth in the Middle East is another aspect of the marginalization of Muslim youth in the

Middle East that contributes to youth marginalization and attraction of extremist and violent organizations.

The problem of youth employment is also evident in many parts of Africa. A recent documentary on the recruitment of Al-Shabab fighters in Kenya shows that these youths were paid up to $500 to join the Al Shabab and then receive a salary of $100 per week as members of the insurgency. Al-Shabab promotes hostility between Christians and Muslims and this leads to fear of the ethnic Somalis who now often live in segregated communities within Kenya. Many of them were radicalized by a Muslim cleric, Sheikh Ahmed Iman Ali, who fled to Somalia in 2009 to act as the Al-Shabab propaganda chief and recruit Kenyans into its military arm. Al Shabab posts propaganda videos on YouTube to capture the minds and hearts of Somali youth.[8] Most of the U.S. effort to counter Al-Shabab has been military in nature and lacks a focused economic development component. Kenya and East Africa do have significant economic resources but have been plagued by corruption and lack of transparency within the government. Kenya has undertaken a major railway project in 2013, with funding from China connecting Mombasa, a key coastal and port city, with Nairobi and then toUganda, Rwanda and South Sudan. Kenya also has a robust private sector with growing access to the Internet. Kenya leads all of Africa for Internet connectivity and access. Over 50% of the Kenya population now has access to the Internet, the highest in all of Africa.

Kenya has achieved a confluence of infrastructure and provision that has positioned it with the highest growth in Internet take-up compared to income per capita in Africa. It has effectively become an outlier in its Internet take-up, and seen Nairobi join Johannesburg as one of Africa's two regional Internet hubs, Kenya is said to have more undersea cables than its peers in the region. The nation boasts of a 20-fold increase in international bandwidth in the country to 20 gigabytes per second. [9] In the Information Age in which we live technology has become one of the major sources for the growth of employment throughout the world. Silicon Valley (San Jose region) and San Francisco lead the nation in job growth, investment and technological innovation. Over 50,000 jobs in the technology sector were created in the Bay Area in

2015. In the Middle East Jordan has become a leader in Internet based technology companies that are becoming an engine of economic growth in the Middle East. Nairobi in East Africa also has the same potential now that Internet access is increasingly ubiquitous in the urban areas of Kenya. Kenya has become a leader in mobile payment technology through its M-Pesa mobile software. Kenya now has the most advanced Internet infrastructure in Africa and could become the leading center for technology development in Africa.

This improved connectivity has helped lay the foundations for Africa's "Silicon Valley" in Nairobi. Dubbed "Silicon Savannah", this is an area in Kenya that has attracted a range of tech start-ups and venture capital firms. International tech giants such as Google, Intel, Nokia and Microsoft have sites in Nairobi and IBM has recently opened a new tower block, the IBM Innovation Centre, which is the company's first research lab in Africa. [10]

As these technology developments take hold in the Middle East and Africa, the educational infrastructure will be needed to train the engineering talent necessary to run these companies and develop the technological innovations appropriate for Africa. It may be necessary for the Western nations to encourage American and European universities to partner with African colleges and universities in the initial stages of their adaptation to the Internet technological revolution.

Technological education will be a key factor in training the youth of the Middle East and Africa to develop business enterprises that will connect the Middle East and Africa to markets throughout the world. It may be a much better investment for Western nations to support the technological education of African youth than putting all of our investments into the military sector. Without the growth of the employment sector the Middle East and Africa will be subject to continued instability and the growing marginalization of large groups of youth in these countries. In Kenya the Somali population generally lives in the most marginalized areas of the country and is subject to discrimination and harassment by the police and military. The lack of educational advancement and limited employment opportunities makes these youths vulnerable to the recruitment efforts by Al-Shabab.

Similar problems exist in North Africa where there is a higher level of educational attainment but a dearth of employment opportunities even for well educated youth. Most of the jobs are in the public sector and what is needed are more jobs in the private sector. The United States government has supported economic development in Tunisia through loan guarantees of over 500 million dollars in 2014 to help Tunisia gain access to capital markets. Information and communications technology is among the fastest growing sectors of Tunisia, Algeria and Palestine in addition to Jordan. If Israel could be brought into a partnership with the rest of the Middle East to further technological development it could be the surest path to peace for Israel and the Arab world which surrounds it.

MENA countries appear to have picked up on this fact: Palestine in recent years has seen the birth of 300 new ICT companies, while Israel "is a start-up nation by now", said Simone Sala, a post-doctoral research fellow at Columbia University. The boom in social networks—with 56 million Arab-speaking users on Facebook—and smartphone applications has given rise to sundry successful applications, which have attracted the attention of the most innovative sector companies.[11]

Teilhard de Chardin correctly envisioned the role that technology and communications would play in shaping the future global society. Even though he lived through World War I and World War II he never lost the sense that the future belonged to those who understood the evolution of humanity toward a deeper interdependence based on a shared moral foundation. Global spiritual leaders such as the Dalai Lama, Thich Nhat Hanh, and Pope Francis have provided us with moral leaderships on many social and environmental issues. The Parliament of World Religions supported the global ethics movement at its 1993 convocation in Chicago.

The Declaration Toward a Global Ethic was drafted by the Roman Catholic theologian, Dr. Hans Kung, and approved by the delegates attending the 1993 Parliament convocation. The core principles of the Global Ethic are stated below:

We women and men of various religions and regions of Earth therefore address all people, religious and non-religious. We wish to express the following convictions which we hold in common: We all have a responsibility for a better global order.

Our involvement for the sake of human rights, freedom, justice, peace, and the preservation of Earth is absolutely necessary.

Our different religious and cultural traditions must not prevent our common involvement in opposing all forms of inhumanity and working for greater humaneness.

The principles expressed in this Global Ethic can be affirmed by all persons with ethical convictions, whether religiously grounded or not.

. . . In such a dramatic global situation humanity needs a vision of peoples living peacefully together, of ethnic and ethical groupings and of religions sharing responsibility for the care of Earth.[12]

The interfaith movement received a major stimulus in 1993 when the Parliament of World Religions met for the first time since 1893 and it has continued to meet regularly since that time with the most recent convocation in November of 2015 in Salt Lake City, Utah. Over 10,000 people attended. The interfaith movement is providing tangible support for the global ethics movement through its emphasis upon an inclusive understanding of religious belief that encompasses all of humanity. The title for the 2015 Parliament expressed well the universality of its message: *Reclaiming the Heart of Our Humanity: Working Together for a World of Compassion, Peace, Justice and Sustainability.* One of the keynote speakers for the Parliament was Dr. Eboo Patel, founder of the Interfaith Youth Corps based in Chicago. He has established interfaith youth projects in India, Sri Lanka and South Africa. He founded the Interfaith Youth Corps in Chicago in 2012. The interfaith Youth Corps sponsors a Leadership Training Institute each summer in Chicago for college students. The challenge ahead of organizations such as the Interfaith Youth Corps will be to train college age students from the Middle East and Africa to reach the areas most affected by interfaith and intercultural conflict.

The United Religion Initiative based in San Francisco has provided an international platform for its interfaith program through its Cooperation Circles which are now located throughout the world. Few of the interfaith organizations have yet had a substantial presence in most of the areas of conflict in the Middle East and North Africa. The Tanenbaum Center for Interreligious Understanding in New York has developed an interreligious curriculum for use in high schools appropriate for a United States and African context that we plan to use in our interfaith training for Kenyan teachers in 2016. *Coexist: A Skills Based Curriculum for Understanding Conflict Resolution* is a one semester curriculum outline that can be adapted to both public and private high schools where many young people have their attitudes formed about interfaith dialogue and understanding. [13] The Coexist curriculum includes a case study on Nigeria which highlights the interfaith transformation that took place there in the relationship between a Pastor and an Imam. In 1999 Imam Ashafa and Pastor James published a significant book entitled *The Pastor and the Imam: Responding to Conflict.*[14] This book highlighted key interfaith texts in both The Bible and the Qur'an. For the Bible we have the following passage:

> "And Peter opened his mouth and said 'Truly I perceive that God shows no partiality, but in every nation anyone who fears God and does what is right is acceptable to God."(Acts 17:28)

> For the Qur'an we have the following passage: "O mankind! We created you from a (pair) of a male and female, and made you into nations and tribes, that

ye may know each other, not that ye may despise each other."(The Qur'an 49:13)

The recognition of pluralism in religious belief has been a major issue in Muslim majority countries since 9/11 and the Iraq War. Christians have either been marginalized in most of the countries where they have lived for centuries or they have had to flee areas such as Iraq and Syria because of the growth of Al Qaeda and ISIS. Similar attacks against Christians have also occurred in West and East Africa where Boko Haram and Al-Shabab have attacked Christians. One of the most encouraging developments in 2016 has been the Marrakesh Declaration which recognizes the rights of religious minorities in Muslim countries. This Declaration came out of a conference held in January, 2016 in Morocco and sponsored by King Mohammad VI of Morocco and the Forum for Promoting Peace in Muslim Societies based in the United Arab Emirates. This gathering brought together over 300 Muslim religious scholars with representatives from diverse religious groups such as Christians, Jews, Bahais, Hindus, Yazidis and Sabeans living in Muslim countries. This conference affirmed the rights of religious minorities by appealing to the Medina Charter.

> The Medina Charter established the idea of common citizenship regardless of religious belief," said Sheikh Abdallah bin Bayyah, a Mauritanian religious scholar and a professor of Islamic studies in Saudi Arabia who helped convene the meeting, in a speech. "Enough bloodshed. We are heading to annihilation. It is time for cooperation.[15]

The conference did establish a framework for religious toleration in countries that recognize that there is an established tradition that goes back to the era of the Prophet Mohammad. Even though extremist groups such as ISIS and Al Qaeda will not recognize the authority of this declaration it will have an impact among moderate religious leaders in the countries that have had an upsurge in religious extremism leading to those groups approving of attacks upon Christians and other religious minorities. The Marrakesh Declaration calls upon Muslim majority countries to follow these principles in relation to the religious minorities living in these countries:

> Call upon Muslim scholars and intellectuals around the world to develop a jurisprudence of the concept of "citizenship" which is inclusive of diverse groups. Such jurisprudence shall be rooted in Islamic tradition and principles and mindful of global changes.

> Urge Muslim educational institutions and authorities to conduct a courageous review of educational curricula that addresses honestly and effectively any material that instigates aggression and extremism, leads to war and chaos, and results in the destruction of our shared societies;

> Call upon politicians and decision makers to take the political and legal steps necessary to establish a constitutional contractual relationship among its citizens, and to support all formulations and initiatives that aim to fortify relations and understanding among the various religious groups in the Muslim World;

> AFFIRM that it is unconscionable to employ religion for the purpose of aggressing upon the rights of religious minorities in Muslim countries

> Marrakesh Declaration adopted on January 27, 2016.[16]

The use of the Internet to combat the Islamic state must be accompanied by other forms of education that deal with the manner in which students understand both their own religion but also critical thinking about how Muslim majority countries have evolved over the centuries and experienced a series of conflicts with the Christian majority countries of Europe and the United States. The level of understanding about the historical development of Islam and Christianity is very much lacking both in the U.S. and Europe but also in the Muslim majority countries. The bias of the Western based educational model fails to understand that the Muslim majority countries continue to view the world through an Islamic faith prism whereas most of the Western nations now view the world through a secular and scientific prism. Part of the conflict between Christianity and Islam has come about because of cultural and political factors that have become epistemological barriers to true dialogue and understanding among members of the two largest religious groupings in the world. Hans Kung, in his magisterial study of Islam, *Islam: Past, Present and Future,* discusses the various images we in the West have about Islam (Hostile, Idealized and Real) and the various paradigms that have existed over the fourteen centuries of Islamic history.

Among these paradigms is the narrative of the Community (Ummah) of Origin. We find certain fundamentalist groups such as the Salafis who identify with the earliest period of Islam which bears similarity with biblical fundamentalists in Christianity who claim that the standard for Christianity must be in the faith and practice of the earliest Christian community. Both the Salafists and the Evangelical Christians tend to promote a literal and more dogmatic view of these religions along with a more puritanical morality. The conflicts within Islam over the past centuries have shaped the present day crisis and given birth to extremist groups such as Al Qaeda and ISIS.

The modern world dominated by science and technology had its origins in the Arab world in the early Middle Ages which influenced the birth of the European university movement of the twelfth and thirteenth centuries. The Arab Empire of the early Middle Ages transferred enormous sums of knowledge to the university based educational systems which developed a particular type of methodology and epistemology allowing science and technology to flourish and leading to the European Renaissance. The decline of science and technology in the Muslim majority countries occurred over a considerable period of time but by the time of the European Renaissance it had lost its position of dominance in these fields of study and transferred its leadership to Western scholars and academics.

Fundamentalism in its various intellectual and religious forms bears at least part of the responsibility for the contemporary intellectual, spiritual and political divides that now exist in the Muslim majority countries and in the United States and Europe. By examining the historical and philosophical sources for this division we can better understand how to transform the divide into a bridge to the future for our youth living today in Muslim majority countries and those living in parts of the world affected by the growth of Christianity. Even though religion does not exist in isolation it does play a formative role in the shaping of the minds of our youth, particularly those living in Muslim majority countries. There is no more important task than the shaping of the minds of the next generation. Educators and religious leaders along with parents bear the most responsibility for this task. The lack of critical thinking about religion and the dearth of historical research on the interaction of the major religious and cultural traditions of Islam and Christianity are part of the gap in knowledge and understanding that plagues our planet today.

Added to this gap in knowledge and understanding is the element of fear and paranoia which pushes members of these faith traditions away from each other and can lead to anger and hostility toward each other. It is the purpose of this book to diagnose the various forces that have pushed us apart but also the way forward to better understanding and appreciation of each other.

In addition to knowledge and understanding of the Other, we also need to develop the skills necessary to teach our youth ways to resolve human conflicts through a process of dialogue, self-understanding and the art of non-judgmental listening that opens new pathways to peace and reconiciliation. The great religions of the world outside of Christianity and Islam also have something to teach us about non-violence and compassion that can lead us forward out of the labyrinth of darkness and chaos into the sunlight of a new day for humanity. From the time of the Renaissance onwards we have had utopian visions of a new society in which all peoples could live together in peace and serenity, but they have yet to be realized by the time of our writing. Nevertheless, the dream of an age of peace among religious believers could portend an age of peace among the nations. Hans Kung has put this very well in the following passage from his study of Islam.

No peace among the nations without peace among the religions

No peace among the religions without dialogue among the religions

No dialogue between the religions without investigation of the foundations of religion. [17]

Reference

1   Teilhard de Chardin, *Building the Earth* (Wilkes-Barre, PA.: Dimension Books, 1965), 54-55.

2   Teilhard de Chardin, *Man's Place in Nature* (New York, Harper and Row, 1956) 110.

3   See the TED talk by Wael Ghonim on the Egyptian Revolution, "Wael Ghonim: Inside the Egyptian revolution."
    March 4, 2011. https://www.youtube.com/watch?v=SWvJxasiSZ8
    See also the book by Wael Ghonim, *Revolution 2.0: The Power of the People is Greater than the People in Power:Memoir* (Mariner Books: 2013).

4   UNICEF demographic data on Egyptian youth: http: www.unicerp.org/inobycountry/Egypt

5   Pierre Teilhard De Chardin, *Human Energy* (London: Harvest Books, 1962), 105

6   Karen Armstrong, *The Great Transformation* (New York: Knopf, 2006) xiii, xiv

7   Karen Armstrong, The Charter for Compassion, http://www.charterforcompassion.org/

8   http://www.soliya.net/?q=what_we_do_connect_program

9   Elayne Wangalwa, CNBC Africa, "Kenya leads Africa's Internet access and connectivity," Sept 24, 2014. http://www.cnbcafrica.com/news/east-africa/2014/09/09/kenya-leads-Internet/

10 http://mgafrica.com/article/2015-02-19-why-kenya-is-africas-tech-hub

11 Nancy Messieh, "Jordan: The Middle East's Silicon Valley," *Middle East*, http://thenextweb.com/me/2011/06/07/jordan-the-middle-easts-*silicon*-valley/#gref

12 Parliament of World Religions, "Declaration Toward a Global Ethic," September 4, 1993.
http://repository.berkleycenter.georgetown.edu/930904KungParliament DeclarationTowardGlobalEthic.pdf

13 *Coexist*, Grades 9-12 (New York: Tanenbaum Center for Interreligious Understanding, 2007)

14 Imam Ashafa and Pastor James, *The Pastor and the Imam: Responding to Conflict* (Muslim/Christian Youth Dialogue Forum: 1999)

15 Aida Alami, "Muslim Conference Calls for Protection of Religious Minorities," *New York Times,* February 2, 2016.

16 Joe Cochrane, "From Indonesia, A Muslim Challenge to the Ideology of the Islamic State," *New York Times*, November 26, 2015.

17 Hans Kung, *Christianity: Essence, History, Future*
http://www.goodreads.com/quotes/157789-no-peace-among-the-nations-without-peace-among-the-religions

Chapter Seven

THE STATE OF CHRISTIAN-MUSLIM RELATIONS IN KENYA
Martin Olando

Kenya is predominantly Christian, with Muslims making up about eleven percent of its population, mostly along the North Eastern parts, its coastal region, and in cities such as Mombasa. Muslims in Kenya largely live along the coast, while the inland population is predominantly Christian except in places such as Mumias. Other faiths practiced in Kenya are African Traditional Religion, and Hinduism. (https://en.wikipedia.org/wiki/Religion_in_Kenya)

Muslims and Christians have a long history of peaceful coexistence in Kenya, compared to countries such as Nigeria and Central Africa Republic, where there has been violence based on religious platforms. Despite being referred to "religious of the book" at times believing in the same prophets and a monotheistic God, Christianity and Islam in Kenya have experienced tensions and differences which recur whenever there are terror attacks.

Kenya is a unique place with regards to Christian-Muslim relations. Amidst the terror attacks on perceived Christian strongholds, the country has never gone to full-blown violence between Muslims and Christians. This could be attributed to commonality in some cultural beliefs between Kenyan Christians and Muslims. There are shared cultural values and the national motto *Harambee,* meaning pulling together, which is anchored in the African *Ubuntu* philosophy. The

Harambee philosophy started by the first president of Kenya, Mzee Jomo Kenyatta rallies all Kenyans to join in fighting poverty, diseases, and illiteracy. The Ubuntu Philosophy includes the essential human virtues—compassion and humanity to others. Compassion and humanity serve as precursors to attaching value to human life irrespective of diverse faith backgrounds. Both Ubuntu and Harambee philosophies have an element of African hospitality, which literally means to help, assist, and to love. As stated by Gathogo, African hospitality combines the following spiritual concepts:

Harambee is a mixture of Swahili and African words. It literally means pulling together, working together towards the same goal, to alleviate Socio-Economic poverty. It is rooted in the tenets of African hospitality (Gathogo; 103, 2001)

African hospitality is crucial in Christian/Muslim relations in Kenya since it reminds the adherents of these faiths that they should love one another because of their African identity and philosophy. In the Kenya coastal towns of Mombasa and Lamu, Muslims and Christians live as neighbors and they work together in response to local problems, such as drought, violence, crime etc., hence creating an image of the "other" as people with whom one can work to better communal life.

Though there had been simmering tension amongst Muslim and Christians, the epitome of the relationship turned into hostility after the terror attacks in 1998 on the American Embassy in Nairobi, the Kikambala attacks, and the Westgate Mall and a host of churches in 2013. The 2014 Mpeketoni attacks and at the University in Garrisa in 2015, where over seventy students mostly from the non–Somali community were killed, further turned the relationship from bad to worse.

In the more recent attack, on 31 January, 2016 in Kenya's coastal Lamu County, four people were killed. Al-Shabaab took credit, telling Al Jazeera Television: "Our fighters attacked non-believers in the occupied Muslim land of Lamu. Our Mujahideen killed several non-believers in the attack. (*World Watch Monitor*, April 1, 2016) The attack on Bishaaro hotel in Mandera, Northern Eastern, where over 12 people were killed, continued to create an impression that Islam is fighting

Christianity. According to a survivor the attackers were shouting "'Allah Akbar, Allah Akbar," meaning God is great (*Daily Nation* October 25, 2016). This only serves to further complicate Christian-Muslim relations since most Christians, either due to ignorance or perception, cannot distinguish between terror attacks and Islam as two different entities. For the lay Christian it becomes an uphill task to understand that there is difference between the terrorist and Islam, which is a religion of peace.

The frequent attacks by terrorists on the Christian establishment gave birth to Islamophobia and hatred and fear towards ethnic communities perceived to be Muslims, namely the Somali, Swahili and Arabs. Islamophobia has resulted in prejudice toward Muslims; Somali and Arab women in hijabs are referred to as terrorists to the extent that they would not share the elevator and public transport with Christians. Further, there is an unwritten rule in some parts of the country that Christians should not be neighbors with Muslims and Christian landlords cannot give tenancy to Muslims. In the aftermath of any terror attacks Islamophobic messages are circulated over social media. Increased levels of prejudice, hatred and discrimination towards Muslims by Christians have become common in Kenya. As a result, there is a new breed of Christian fundamentalism growing in Kenya, making the efforts to bring about religious tolerance more complex and difficult.

Islamophobia has many side effects as described by the Runnymede Trust, the UK's leading independent race equality think tank group. The Runnymede Trust emphasizes how Islamophobia affects youngsters in violent forms, for example, as social disorders. This is evident when trends such as gang-formation take shape: consisting of criminality and territorial traits. Social rejection might lead to a growing drug addiction and criminality among Muslims, which in the end could cause riots such as the one in France 2005. (Runnymede; 18: 1997) (http://theamericanmuslim.org). In the coastal town of Mombasa, Islamophobia might be the cause of radicalization and a high rate of insecurity in parts of the Majengo, Kisauni estate and the Old Town, where gang-wielding youths attack people.

Despite the attacks and suspicion, Muslims have stood with the Christians in the midst of the attacks to show the correct relationship that Islam preaches. During an attack by the militant group, Al Shabaab on Christians, a group of Muslim passengers shocked Al-Shabaab fighters who had ambushed a bus travelling from Nairobi to the town of Mandera in December, 2015. The fighters asked Muslims to separate from Christians. Muslim passengers responded saying, "Kill them together (with us) or leave them alone." One of those Muslim passengers, a teacher, Salah Farah, who was shot and later died in the hospital, was posthumously awarded one of Kenya's top honors (http://www.bbc.co.uk/news, December 21,2015). Muslim leaders from the Bishaaro Mandera area strongly condemned the attacks on the Bishaaro hotel, terming the killings "bizarre, heinous and "barbaric" while consoling the bereaved. (*Daily Nation* 5, October 26, 2016.)

Despite efforts to restore faith and trust among Christians and Muslims, there is still suspicion in some areas. In the Mikunumbi Secondary school, in the Mpeketoni area of Lamu, where over 70 people were killed in June, 2014, the number of Christians students attending the school has been sharply reduced. The school had over 400 students of which 150 were Christians and 250 Muslims. Two years after the attack there are only 45 Christians students— a clear indication that despite many peace efforts suspicion is rife. Francis Njuguna, who retired from his post as deputy head teacher at Mkunumbi Secondary School, says that many Christians are reluctant to send their children to the school because they don't trust their Muslim neighbors. (Interview, Francis Njuguna, Retired deputy Teacher, Mkunumbi secondary school, 2015)

Fundamentalism exists amongst Christian and Muslim groupings. Public debates known as *Mihadhara,* where there are discussions about Christian and Islamic key doctrines, ignite hatred and hostility. Though *Mihadharas* are becoming less frequent, they provide an avenue for confrontation. It is common in *Mihadhara* to hear claims that Jesus is not the son of God, a concept advanced by an Islamic preacher. A Christian attendee would refute that. In many instances the public debates draw a huge crowd in which many in attendance may not be conversant with either Islam or Christian teachings. As Mutei asserts: the practice of *mihadhara* (confrontational street preaching) by Muslims in Kenya has become a form of both actual and symbolic confrontation, as Muslim speakers seek to discredit the Christian scriptures and Christianity, often by reinterpreting Christian scriptures to support their own conclusions (Mutei, 2012). *Midhara* turns out to be a superiority contest in public and some of the participants often have poor knowledge of the orthodox teachings found either in Islam or Christianity.

Christian leaders have openly expressed their fears on behalf of the people they lead.

> "There is a lot of fear," Father Wilybard Lagho, Vicar General of the Catholic Diocese of Mombasa, told the *Christian Science Monitor* in January. "The level of tolerance that has been there since the two religions were founded has, in the last 20 years, been challenged by incidents (http://www.csmonitor.com/World Africa, January 2015, 0329)

Wherever there is an attack there are increased fears and talks of protection, with some pastors asking to be given guns during church services in anticipation of any attacks. Many big churches throughout the country conduct service under watch of armed police guard, a scenario that had not been witnessed until 2011 after the Kenya military incursion into Somalia.

The suspicion between Muslims and Christians in Kenya also can be attributed to a lack of knowledge among the followers of these religions. Many doctrinal issues and differences could be best handled by informed religious leaders. For example, the "Abuja Declaration" which was made during a meeting in Nigeria in 1989, stated the goal of a group of Muslim religious leaders to " . . . make Islam the Religion of Africa" (https://en.wikipedia.org/wiki/Abuja_Declaration, 1989). The Abuja Declaration noted that Muslims in Africa had been deprived of their rights to be governed under sharia laws which should be re-introduced. The Abuja declaration brought fear among Kenyan Christians, and during the referendum for the Kenyan Constitution in 2010 it was used to rally Christians to vote NO change for the Constitution. The misunderstanding of the Abuja Declaration always crops up as a contentious issue in Christian-Muslim dialogue. The Kenyan Constitution, like any other in the world, recognizes that the minority populations should be given equal treatment. Muslims are the minority in a country where Christianity dominates, and due to the constitutional requirement many Muslims now occupy top positions in the government. These constitutional appointments are used by some Christians to further their argument that the Abuja declaration will come to pass. Human rights were a key component of the Kenya Constitution in 2010. Prior to 2010, Muslim youths were arrested and some would disappear without a trace on suspicion of being terrorists or terrorist sympathizers. Today terror suspects have their rights and they appear in court like any other suspect. This has eased the relationship between Muslims and Christians, because there is less victimization of suspects and the terror victims feel that justice has been done.

The Kenyan educational system is geared towards segregating religious groups. For instance, there exist both Christian Religious Education (CRE) and Islamic Religious Education (IRE) During these lessons students are grouped by their religious identity and this separation tends to alienate the young people from each other. There has been discussion on the need to have Kenyan schools become secular, but none of the parents of either Muslims or Christians want to hear that because, according to Mbiti, Africans are an essentially religious people. If Kenyan schools were made secular, that might help to change this perception. As advanced by Rukyaa, schooling is a fundamental part of life for most Kenyan children, a time when ideas are learned and reproduced. Many have insisted that public schools should be made secular, not Christian (Rukyaa 200-202). As an alternative, there could be a curriculum change that would include the principles of interfaith dialogue and interfaith studies in both primary and secondary schools. By emphasizing these interfaith principles at a very young age, religious extremism would be largely avoided and religious cooperation emphasized.

Despite the religious tension and hostility in Kenya there are varies grassroots interfaith peace-building initiatives and organizations that have been working hard to foster coexistence. Most of these groups use religion to encourage peaceful relations since it connects deeply with social and cultural norms of a society. There have been a lot of misconceptions about the dialogue between Christians and Muslims. Extremists in both Islam and Christianity think that the dialogue is about conversion. Many interfaith dialogues bear less fruit because of a lack of understanding. Dialogue is about both Christians and Muslims holding on to their faith but at the same time respecting the other's point of view. According to the World Council of Churches' guidelines on dialogue with people of living faiths and ideologies, "Dialogue means witnessing to our deepest convictions, whilst listening to those of our neighbors" (Cited, Bosch,1991:484). Dialogues should not be superiority contests or opportunities to demonize the other's faith but, rather, forums in which to develop a deeper understanding of each other's faith.

The Catholic Church in Kenya publishes a religious magazine, *Come closer*. The objective of the magazine is to create the awareness among Christians about various teachings of Islam and Christianity. The main purpose of the publication is to continue bridging the gap between Muslims and Christians while stressing the need for dialogue, thus showing the practicality of the *Nostra Acetate* document of Vatican II that the "authentic dialogue is witness and genuine evangelization is realized in respect and attentiveness towards others" (*Ibid*, P.221)

Groups such as the Coast Interfaith Council of Clerics (CICC) and Global Ministries University (GMU based in USA) are, among many others, carrying out several activities to enhance Christian/Muslim relations in Kenya. Kenya needs peace and it is not lost to all that after the 2007 post election violence there was resurgence of peaceful activities. The Kenyan populace, whether Muslim or Christian, has common enemies, namely corruption, lack of clean drinking water, access to medical facilities, unemployment, and lack of security, among many other problems.

The Interfaith peace groups have engaged in a series of empowering activities among young people by providing them with entrepreneurial skills. It is the young people of Islam and Christianity who are mostly vulnerable and are exploited in order to cause violence in the name of religion. With entrepreneurial skills they can earn a living and take control of their lives rather than be driven by selfish war mongers to join militia groups and unleash terror attacks. Any idle mind stands a high chance of indoctrination through religion since, as stated by Karl Marx, religion can be the opium of the masses and can be used to cultivate hatred towards different faiths.

The teachings of Islam and Christianity can lay a foundation for interfaith dialogue. Religious faith plays a key role in influencing human thinking. It guides one's perspective of reality and judgment, which is crucial in fashioning value systems (Tarimo, 21, 2005). Islam and Christianity both teach about loving one's neighbor. Jesus Christ is quoted on several occasions where He reminds His followers to love thy neighbor and do good. The Parable of the Good Samaritan illustrates that irrespective of race, color, ethnicity and religious affiliation a Christian should do good to all. A neighbor is the person next to you irrespective of religious or economic status. Bosch describes that the Parable of the Good Samaritan teaches about inclusiveness, dissolving alienation and bridging gaps between Christians and other people. (Bosch,1991:28)

It is a well-known fact that Islamic teachings such *Al Tawhid* (Unity of Being), *Afu* (forgiveness), *Rahmah* (compassion) and *Rahim* (mercy) illustrate concepts of peace. Qur'anic verses such as the one cited below should help build relationships between Muslims and Christians:

> The same religion, He has established for you as that which he enjoined on Noah-that Which We have sent by inspiration to thee—and that which We enjoined on Abraham, Moses and Jesus; Namely, that you should remain steadfast in religion and make no Divisions therein . . . (42:13)

The interfaith dialogue groups have demystified some theological and imaginary issues which have haunted Christian-Muslim relations.

These interfaith initiatives encourage sharing of Christian and Muslim festivals. Kenya is a spiritual country with many religious festivals. There are major Christian and Muslim festivals: for Christians, namely Christmas, Easter and Good Friday, whereas for the Muslims we have *Id al-Fitr* and *Id al-Adha*. Initially, the country had only reserved the *Id il-Fitr* as a public holiday. The Muslim community intensified its request to declare *Id al-Adha* as a public holiday and it was granted. Celebration of *Id al-Adha* as a public festival has created an atmosphere in which the Muslim community feels that they are treated on a par with Christians. The gesture by the Kenyan government has helped dispel some of the tension over inequality or unfair treatment towards Islam.

Peace between Muslim and Christians in Kenya has continued to develop. It is very common to see Mosques and Churches painted yellow in some parts of Nairobi. To a layperson this can appear as an artistic impression to beautify places of worship. However, this is a concept of "The Colour in Faith" developed by artist Yazmany Arboleda as a way of demonstrating a shared humanity which is irrespective of different faiths. The painting is done by both Muslims and Christians together as an expression of love and evidence that, despite their religious differences, they are people belonging to one Creator. Arboleda says the act of painting the buildings has brought different communities together. "To see people smile and talk to each other is beautiful". (http://www.christiantoday.com/article/churches.and.mosques).

Suspicions and barriers on interfaith marriage especially between Muslims and Christians always evoke emotions. According to Islam, a Muslim woman is formally forbidden to marry a non-Muslim man, regardless of his religion, while a Muslim man is allowed to get married to a non-Muslim woman. For the Christian it is forbidden to be yoked with a non–believer, interpreted loosely that a Christian cannot marry from another faith. (In an interfaith seminar held in Mombasa, participants, both Muslim and Christians, strongly objected to the idea of interfaith marriage.). This represents a view of the majority of Christians and Muslims who enjoy interfaith dialogue but can never imagine the marriage between a Muslim and a Christian. This scenario is a replica of the social relationship between Muslims and Christians in Kenya.

Both Christianity and Islam in Kenya should teach tolerance and emphasize the image of God in everyone. This would make the young people understand and embrace their cultural and spiritual identity since all human beings share essentially the same humanity. Personality is formed at an early age and educational formation plays a key role in the structure of one's adult life. An open and inclusive attitude developed at a young age can eliminate the tendency to religious seclusion and animosity toward those outside of one's faith community.

Muslims and Christians need to put aside their theological differences in order to save young people from being radicalized by terrorist groups which form a small minority among the Muslim population. Christians and Muslims have much to gain from solidarity with each other which will allow them to grow together in a peaceful civil society.

References

Islamophobia a challenge for us all', Commission on British Muslims and Islamophobia, The Runnymede Trust, 1997, UK.

Bosch, D.J 1991. *Transforming Mission: Paradigm Shifts in Theology of Mission.* Orbis Books, Maryknoll New York

Gathogo, Julius.2001. *The Truth about African Hospitality is there Hope for Africa?* The Salt Production, Mombasa, Kenya.

Rukyaa, Julian J. "Muslim-Christian Relations in Tanzania with Particular Focus on the Relationship between Religious Instruction and Prejudice." *Islam and Christian–Muslim Relations* 18.2 (2007): 189-204. Print

Tarimo, Aquiline. 2005. *Applied Ethics and Africa's Social Reconstruction.* Acton Publishers, Nairobi.Kenya.

Mutei, J. M. (2012). *Mihadhara as a Method of Islamic Da'wah in Kenya: An Analysis of Inter-Religious Dialogue in a Proselytizing Context.* Nairobi: Nairobi Academic Press.

Wamue, Grace, Theuri Mathew, ed. 2003. *Quests for Integrity in Africa.* Acton Publishers, Nairobi, Kenya

(https://en.wikipedia.org/wiki/Abuja_Declaration_(1989)

(http://www.christiantoday.com/article/churches.and.mosques).

(https://en.wikipedia.org/wiki/Religion_in_Kenya)

Ethnic cleansing' plaguing Christians in Kenya, World Watch Monitor,
      April1, 2016

(www\\ bbc.co.uk/news, December,21,2015).

Chapter Eight

GÜLEN-INSPIRED SCHOOLS AND THEIR CONTRIBUTION TO CHRISTIAN-MUSLIM RELATIONS IN NAIROBI, KENYA

Fatih Akdogan, Mombasa, Kenya

Abstract

This chapter serves to examine how Gülen-inspired Light Academy Schools contribute peaceful and constructive Christian-Muslim relations in Kenyan society based on Gülen's educational and dialogue ideas. This is a case study of Nairobi Light Academy Boys Secondary School due to it being the oldest and the biggest amongst other branches of Light Academy Schools. Located in Nairobi, the capital city, the school enrolls students from all over Kenya. Through this scope, the researcher was able to observe the impact of the schools on Kenyan society. The methodology included in-depth interviews, focused group discussions and questionnaires. Compared to other African countries, Kenya is one of the most peaceful countries in terms of the respect accorded to the respective faith of others. Christians and Muslims comprise more than 90 percent of the entire population of Kenya. It cannot be asserted that Christian-Muslim Relations are ideal. In order to promote peaceful co-existence, positive and constructive relations are necessary amongst the adherents of both religions. Education could be an equalizer and can be used to promote interfaith dialogue.

The schools in Kenya could be classified into three categories: private, religious, and public. Most of the religious schools require that students adhere to their own forms of worship regardless of the students' faith and denomination. Many people prefer these schools due to various factors such as academic performance, availability of scholarships, and convenience. In this respect, beliefs are ignored for the sake of one's future. Consequently, those students are either converted, or a majority of them graduate with negative feelings for other faiths that turn out to be an obstacle to interfaith dialogue. While the same situation prevails in private schools, depending on the owner, public schools seem to be neutral. Light Academy attempts to be a well-balanced school that treats students fairly in terms of their religious beliefs and ethnicity. In this study, we see in practice how Gülen's educational and dialogue theories are implemented and could be a ground for positive Christian-Muslim Relations in Kenyan society.

Schools have been used as tools to spread or to teach one's religion particularly in African countries. Many schools in Kenya are either sponsored and run by religious groups or by owners who belong to a particular denomination/community and thus reflect the belief of the owner.

The missionary schools have played an important role in the spread of Christianity. Africa became Christian to the extent that its children went to school. In figures, 80-90% of all Christians may have been converted in those schools (Baur 2009, 370). Because of that, Muslims perceived Christian missionary schools as baits for converting their children to Christianity. (Kahumbi, Christian-Muslim Relations in Kenya 1995, 116-141)

Christianity and Islam are the two major religions composing almost two thirds of the world's population; without their peaceful cooperation it is not possible to tackle the global problems of the world and maintain peaceful co-existence. Kenya is one of the most peaceful countries in the African continent and in order to maintain this atmosphere, positive Christian–Muslim relations are needed now more than ever.

Fethullah Gülen (b.1941) is one of the most important thinkers and activists of the Muslim world. He has been promoting interfaith and intercultural dialogue from early 1990s. He gathered people from all walks of life in Turkey in order to have constructive relations. His ideas of love and dialogue have now spread to global levels and inspired many to establish schools and dialogue institutions. The first Gülen-inspired schools opened in Kenya in 1998. This chapter analyzes whether those schools are balanced or not in terms of religious co-existence and the impact of those schools in Kenyan Society in promoting peaceful co-existence. A comparison also made with other schools in Kenya.

2.1 Methodology

What follows is a case study focusing on Gülen-inspired schools in Nairobi. These schools are known in Kenya as Light Academy Schools. The focus for this study is the Light Academy Secondary School since it is the oldest and biggest compared to other branches. The target group for this study is the students whose ages are between 16 to 18. The research obtained comprised of data collected from teachers, non-teaching staff, students graduates and parents. In order to have a balanced research and to be able to compare the findings of the study, the researcher collected some data from various high schools in Kenya.

The researcher used both quantitative and qualitative research methods to answer the research questions, applying in-depth interviews, focused group discussions, semi-structured questionnaires and review of secondary data in order to evaluate the role of the schools in Christian Muslim relations. Snowballing technique (non-probability sample) was used to find those who were present and worked during the establishment of the schools. Students selected from Light Academy Secondary through the systematic method were involved in responding to the questionnaires. While the teachers were interviewed voluntarily, the parents were chosen and interviewed at random during the parents' day. Content analysis was used in order to interpret and analyze the coded and quoted data that was collected through in-depth interviews, questionnaires, and other random sampling methods.

3.1 Gülen's Theory of Education and Dialogue

According to Gülen, the main duty and purpose of human life is to seek understanding. The effort of doing so, known as education, is a perfecting process though which we earn, in the spiritual, intellectual, and physical dimensions of our beings, the rank appointed for us as the perfect pattern of creation (2009: 202). Seemingly, Gülen is trying to create a new generation through educational activities based on universal religious values that would create mutual understanding among the adherents of different faiths and cultures. He simply describes his dream as "Golden Generation" (Celik 2005). This is how we can save our world from wars and hatred and instill love among the people. Therefore, those schools all around the world inspired by him are expected to be affiliated with those ideas.

Gülen believes that many people could be teachers but only a few can educate (Gülen, http://www.fethullahgulen.org/ 2006). To him teaching means seeking academic progress while educating refers to inculcating good character and instilling moral values. Therefore, a teaching post should not only be taken as a job alone but also as a divine duty and thus being a good sample is necessary. The study has shown that 85 % of the Turkish teachers admitted that teaching was their first choice and, for the remaining 15%, their second. Seemingly, Turkish teachers are very much inspired with Gülen's emphasis of teaching since most of them graduated from top universities such as Bogazici, ODTU in Turkey and could easily get lucrative jobs and yet volunteered to come and serve in Kenya. The study shows that though the schools are affiliated with Gülen's ideas, very few people know about him.

Table1: Number of the questionnaires in the study

	Number of respondents	Christians	Know Gülen	Muslims	Know Gülen
Students	50	29	9	21	17
Graduates	25	15	4	10	8
Parents	25	16	3	9	4

Figure 1: The percentage of respondents who know Gülen and read his books.

As it is seen from the graph above, Muslim and Christian respondents are contradictory to each other. Although the school hosts conferences and Gülen's books are easy to access in the school, the number of Christian respondents familiar with Gülen's teachings was very low compared to Muslim respondents. The graph indicates high percentages of Muslim students know Gülen and that many of them read his books. This might be attributed to Gülen's Islamic books that could be used as a religious resource for Muslim students. The religious education teacher Mehmet expressed that he encourages his students to read Gülen's books because they help them to understand the peaceful Islam (Mehmet 15th May 2012).

Additionally, when students, graduates and parents were asked to give their opinion on Gülen's influence in the school, 64% of the respondents believed that he does not have influence in the school. This shows that Gülen's ideas are not exposed in the school.

Figure 2: The percentage of Gülen's influence in school.

65% of the Kenyans' teachers responded that they know about Gülen but only 20 % percent of them read his books. Those respondents who were not aware of Gülen were mostly teachers who have worked with Light Academy for less than 3 years. Teacher Elizabeth, who has been part of the schools since its inception, describes Gülen as a bridge between Islam and Christianity. His understanding of religious tolerance is being practiced in school. Teacher Dancan, a graduate of Light Academy who studied in Turkey and later became a teacher, takes Gülen as a "magnet" between different faiths. He added that the school has helped him to be tolerant of other faiths.

Gülen sees science and faith as not only compatible but also complementary. He further explains that science and religion are like wings of a bird meaning one cannot do without the other (fgulen.com, http://fgulen.org/ 2012). Therefore, the schools inspired by Gülen are expected to be based on a combination of science and faith.

The researcher observed that the school has five science laboratories and hosts a number of Science Olympians. In addition, it has been showing good academic performance, competing with most top schools in Kenya. It secured second position among private schools and ninth nationwide in the Kenyan national exam in 2007. The school also produced the first and the third student nation-wide in the Kenyan national examination in 2011. On the other hand, the school greatly emphasizes character education and moral values through special and unique social activities such as tea talks, parent visits and sleepovers. By so doing, the school is marrying well with its motto that is to bring forth a generation which is morally upright, socially responsible and academically competent. Therefore, this is a reflection of Gülen's education theory.

According to the study, although Light Academy schools are affiliated to Gülen's ideas, there is neither direct teaching of Gülen to the students or parents nor portraits of Gülen to show respect or honor. However, hanging in the corridors are several portraits with quotes written by Gülen and many others about universal values, though names are not written on them. It is possible that what is being said is more important than who said it.

3.2 Implementation of Gülen's Theories

The first Gülen-inspired school volunteers, Mr. Omer and Mr. Mehmet, arrived in Kenya in September 1996. They were first welcomed by Mr. Mahmut whose sister was studying in Turkey. He introduced them to the appropriate people in order to register a trust and to put up a school. In the beginning, he had some doubts since they were very young—in their early 20s and did not know English. He later found them determined and dedicated enough to initiate such a project (Mahmut 26th July 2012). Finally, they did establish the Omeriye Educational and Medical Foundation Charitable Trust in 1997.

Omeriye Foundation is the mother of all Gülen-inspired relief and educational activities. Light Academy, as one of its institutions, was established to fulfill the educational mission in Kenya. The school opened its doors in April 1998 with only 25 students, along Ngong road behind the Uchumi supermarket in Nairobi. The first headmaster was Mr. Ilhan Erdogan, the first teachers were Mr. Turfan, Mr. Kenan and

Mr. Mesut. Jabir, one of the first students, recalls vividly those days and says:

> ". . . indeed there was a lot of excitement in the school
> due to a small number of students. I also remember the
> headmaster; he was a model teacher, father of the school
> and more so respected by all." (Jabir 18th July 2012)

At its inception, Light Academy offered only the 8.4.4 system. In order to accommodate students from all backgrounds and other parts of the world, the school introduced the International General Certificate of Secondary Education (IGCSE) system, which was started in September 2001. In the very same year, the Omeriye Foundation opened another school in Mombasa-Nyali offering local 8.4.4 system and later IGCSE. A year later, the Foundation opened a primary school in Nairobi-Lavington.

The 8.4.4 is a Kenyan system, which entails extensive reading and work that is more theoretical than practical. It is mostly preferred because it is relatively cheap and common to almost all schools. The IGCSE on the other hand is a British system developing one's career from the early age. It is more practical than theoretical. Most of its learners are foreigners and high profile Kenyans who can afford education abroad since this system is recognized internationally by almost all universities.

The atmosphere did not provide ample learning environment at Ngong road due to its nearness to Kibera, the second largest slum in Africa, and the ever busy Ngong road. In addition to this, the school lacked space as the buildings used were rented old town houses. Hence, Mr. Mehmet Ali, an architect from Turkey's Antalya province, during his visit to Kenya with a group of businessmen, thought that the school did not represent the face of their goal that is to serve humanity through education. As a result, Mr. Mehmet Ali and a group of businessmen from Turkey-Antalya decided to buy land to accommodate a school that would carry the real image of Light Academy. They managed to get a 10-acre piece of land at the prestigious Karen and donated to Omeriye Foundation in 2004. The construction did not start until 2007 due to long land-acquiring procedures. They also sponsored the construction costs as well as volunteered in the construction. (Bilge 18th May 2012). A modern school with state-of-the-art facilities was built. The school has 31 well-furnished classrooms, 3 well-equipped science laboratories and 2 computer laboratories with 58 computers connected to the Internet. A campus-like library with a variety of books, five-star dormitories with carpet from the entrance point, a superb modern auditorium with a capacity of 480 and a kitchen with capacity of 400 able to serve a minimum of 2000 people a day. The school has social facilities, both artificial and natural turf fields, and serenely landscaped grounds. The school was officially opened by His Excellency Mr. Abdullah Gul, the President of the Republic of Turkey on 21st February, 2009.

According to teachers Tunc and Were, who witnessed the transformation, the change was remarkable. During their visit with Mr. Tufan, the then-headmaster as the construction was wrapping up, they noted that it would not be fair to compare the two schools since they are in two different worlds. They added that one of the teachers asked the headmaster why the administration preferred putting a dining hall in the middle of the school. Actually, the teacher was referring to the installation of the new school that was two times bigger than the dining hall in the old school (Tunc&Were 2nd July 2012).

The researcher has found that Mombasa Light Academy has also undergone the same transformation. Both secondary and primary sections started in 2001 and 2003 respectively in rented houses. Later on, the donors bought land, as there was need to update and expand the school and to equip it with better and necessary learning equipment due to increased demand of education. A systematic construction method was adopted, as the learning process could not be stopped (Altindis 14th June 2012). By 2010, both schools were complete and opened by Honorable Raila Odinga, the Prime Minister of Kenya on 19th February 2011. During the opening ceremony, he said:

"I take this opportunity to thank Light Academy schools
for the contribution in enhancing academic standards
in Kenya and firmly state that this goes a long way in

helping Kenya fulfill her professional commitments and aspiration of the vision 2030" (LightAcademy 2011).

The school had made a tremendous change in a short period due to the increased demand. It swiftly adapted the Kenyan educational system and made great strides in increasing academic excellence. The school also attracted the attention of prominent personalities among government officials.

3.3 Administration Structure

Omeriye Foundation is the umbrella of all Gülen-inspired relief and educational activities. Therefore, the chairperson of the foundation is also the head of the schools. However, he is assisted by two deputy directors, one who is in charge of academics and the other who deals with non-academic matters. The deputy director in charge of academics heads all six schools in Kenya. He meets with all principals and deputies to discuss academic progress as well as the character development of the students.

The Nairobi boys' secondary has a different administration structure since it offers both systems and accommodates nearly 400 students of which 280 are boarders.

The secondary school has a coordinator in each system. Their work, other than teaching, is to oversee the examinations both internal and external, follow up student attendance, maintain discipline in the school, and analyze the results. They are also a direct source of the school's academic progress as they keep all the results.

Each class has a teacher who is in charge of students' academic performance and character development. He organizes all the social activities such as sleepovers, tea talks, trips, parent visits, etc. However, class teachers in school have no administrative responsibilities compared to many other high schools in Kenya. This enables them to be effective, as they have fewer responsibilities freeing them to have close links with students as well as having fewer students to attend to, at the same time eliminating fear of punishment if the teacher was an administrator. The research shows that the defined duties among the teaching staff and administration enable the later to be effective and available to serve students easily and more quickly whenever possible. Most of the students responded that they can access the headmaster's office without any problem and can discuss whatever they want with the head teacher at a personal level or approach their class teacher or supervisors who are always available. In a cluster of six students, a student revealed that the former head teacher, Mr. Murat, had announced in the assembly that his office doors are open any time to any student and they should not fear to share any problem or opinion they would wish him to solve or know respectively. Seemingly, the school administration is easy to access and the students do so easily.

The school has two dormitory masters, one for each system, to maintain orderliness in the boarding facilities. The school also has supervisors (*belletmen*) who help the dorm masters and class teachers in monitoring the students and their character education. They are university students, most of them from Turkey, who came to study in education facilities. They ensure good studying environment for students during their private study hours, and remind students about punctuality, cleanliness, hard work, discipline, and respect towards each other.

Figure 3: The percentage of the importance of supervisors

The research has shown that the majority (60%) of the interviewed students considers supervisors to be very useful due the roles they play in the dormitory. They describe their role as helping in times of emergencies, guidance, and creating a study atmosphere and assisting them in their academics.

Those who did not find supervisors useful mostly describe them as 'in charge of dorm rules'. However, 84% of the graduates find supervisors useful and describe their roles as necessary; they could easily pass on complaints or seek help from their teacher or administration through these supervisors, .99% of the parents agree that supervisors are not only important but also necessary; seemingly it gives them confidence that their sons and daughters are under care all the time as well as connecting them with their children, as they are not allowed phones in school.

3.4 Academics

According to the interviews done with teachers, priority is given to academic performance rather than the structure or the faith of the school. Teacher Otieno for instance, like seven other respondents, stated that he didn't mind sending his son to a missionary school, even though he knew his son would be forced to worship according to that particular school's faith, simply because the school performance was high (Otieno 21th May 2012).

In the research, more than 80% of interviewees had chosen Light Academy because of its academic performance and facilities offered. On the other hand, some parents in in-depth-interviews said that they had learned about Light Academy from other parents who advised them that the school also placed emphasis on moral values and respect for others, and gave freedom of worship to students from all faiths. Indeed, this is in line with the school motto:

> We are committed to delivering morally upright, socially responsible and academically competent individuals to the society (Light Academy 2012).

Light Academy has made long strides in academic performance within a very short time, as reported by most interviewees. The school prepared students for the national examination in 2001 for the first time and had secured no ranking at all in the academic order of performances. However, 6 years later, the school managed to secure position two among private schools and position nine nationally sending 57 out of 58 students to universities (Mwangi 12th June 2012).

Mr. Gurhan, the former deputy academic director, explained that the school management organizes teachers' workshops every term at Light Academy Karen campus. The workshops bring together departmental teachers from all six branches in order to discuss challenges faced in the subjects and come up with relevant solutions as well as setting goals for the following academic terms. In these workshops, teachers in the same department get an opportunity to teach fellow teachers; relevant teaching approaches are adopted to find the best way of teaching students in class. Each department also agrees on the topics from which a common examination will be set and results to be compared (Gurhan 29th May 2012).

The administration encourages the half-boarding system, meaning students go home on Saturday afternoons and report back on Sunday evenings, unlike other schools that allow students to go home only during midterms and end terms. Although other schools might have strict rules that do not allow even parents to see their child whenever they want, Mr. Engin, the headmaster, states that the school administration believes parents should have adequate time with their children to see them grow morally upright and have time to check on their academic progress. This system helps eliminate homesickness, and any change of behavior noted is corrected in a timely manner. This has led to some schools adopting the same system (Engin 13th July 2012). According to Gülen, in order to have children who are an epitome of success and good morals, parents should have sufficient time with their children as they grow to monitor and guide them (2009: 207). Thus, a triangle of success—student, parent and school—is created.

3.4.1 Olympiads (Scientific Competitions)

The Light Academy has been participating in many different international Olympiad competitions since 2000. Students from different backgrounds are given opportunities to represent the school in these Olympiads. The school meets most of the expenses for the preparation and participation. Seemingly, Olympiads are a tradition of the school and are given much more emphasis compared to other schools in Kenya. For instance, this year, the school took part in seven different Olympiad competitions in four different countries with a total of thirty-one students.

3.4.2 Turkish Olympiad

Turkish Olympiad is one of the many international Olympiad competitions attended by Light Academy. This has given most students opportunities to participate in many categories (Turkish dance, songs, poems and grammar) winning awards for the school as well as individual prizes. According to Mark, Zoram and Ali, while in the competition all participating students had an opportunity to stay with different Turkish families. They learned the Turkish culture, and the Turkish hosts learned about the students' culture. As long as they were in Turkey, their religious choice was respected and all were able to pray as they would do at home (Mark&Zoram&Ali 12th July 2012).

3.4.3 Golden Climate International Environmental Olympiads

Light Academy started hosting an international science Olympiad in 2011 called the Golden Climate International Environmental Project Olympiad. According to teacher Akkilic, the initiator and coordinator, the chief concern is to address environmental challenges like pollution, conservation of energy, re-using or recycling etc., through basic science, engineering and management (Akkilic 29th July 2012).

Mr. Adan, the deputy secretary in the Ministry of Education, declared that this is the first international science Olympiad ever organized and hosted in Kenya (Adan 26th July 2012). Alkali also revealed that, having attended many international competitions, he realized that such a competition was missing in Eastern Africa.

In this way, students from all over the world, particularly from Africa, were given an opportunity to explore their talents and to promote an environmentally conscious generation (Akkilic 29th July 2012).

In the second year, the project gained popularity. The number of participating countries and projects submitted doubled. The project hosted 10 countries with over 50 participants and 35 projects selected for the finals. It has also attracted government officials. For example, the Prime Minister, Hon Raila Odinga, recognized Golden Climate as a project seeking to bring solutions to environmental challenges, and thus sent a commendation letter about this project. In addition to this Mrs. Lily Sambu, the director of Foreign Service in Ministry of Foreign Affairs, referred to the project in her speech as a unique science competition, the only one of its kind in Eastern and Central Africa (Sambu 9th June 2012).

Light Academy also has a very successful drama club that represented the school and won the best and the most coveted trophy, "The best secondary school" in the country, and this was followed by eight other national trophies. The club is made up of 18 students and happens to have an almost equal number of students from both faiths. Joseph, the drama teacher, believes that the success of their drama club is due to the Muslim and Christian prayers they do together before any performances, rehearsals or stage performances. In this way, mutual understanding and brotherhood is created (Joseph 15th June 2012).

Calvin, a recent graduate and a member of the club, admitted that free and open practice of religion together helped them to understand and respect each other's faiths (Calvin 31th July 2012). Paul also said that the club has given him an opportunity to travel across the country meeting various students from diverse cultures. He believes he has gained the ability to relate to and understand people from different cultures and faiths, after all his adventures with the club (Paul 17th June 2012).

3.5 Gülen-Inspired Schools and Their Contribution to Christian-Muslim Relations

According to the researcher, some Muslims consider Light Academy to be a Muslim school since practicing of Islam is allowed and its administrators are Turkish Sunni Muslims. When Light Academy was ranked the top ninth school nationwide, the Muslim weekly magazine *Friday Bulletin* announced its success as a Muslim School (FridayBulletin 2007). On the other hand, many Muslims contend that Light Academy is not a Muslim school since Islamic subjects are not taught.

In a cluster of five Muslim students done on the 24th of June 2012, some students expressed their reasons as to why they think Light

146

Academy is not a Muslim school. One said it is not, since there is no mosque in the school; another said Muslim students are not allowed to be in Muslim dress, *kanzu*. Yet another said that it is not an Islamic school since even Islamic Religious Education is not offered in the school and they are not allowed to read prayers aloud.

In a cluster of five Christian students held on 1st July 2012, a student expressed that Light Academy is a just a secular and private school. Talking in terms of religion, then, it could be said to be a multi-religious school because it admits students from all faiths and gives priority to universal moral values without being guided by a particular faith or denomination. Another student added that no Islamic event, apart from those known worldwide, are celebrated in the school, or allowed to interfere with normal learning, and no Islamic prayers are performed in the presence of students of other faiths, for instance in the assembly. On the contrary, one student argues that Light Academy is a Muslim school since *Jumu'ah* prayers are taken seriously and students are encouraged to pray by the IRE teacher who comes from the primary section to conduct the prayer.

In addition, students were questioning why the number of the Muslim students has been increasing particularly in the British Curriculum. Seemingly, this was true since the school temporarily hosts 24 students in the Kenyan system, all Muslims from interior of North Eastern Kenya sponsored by a Turkish Charitable Organization "*Kimse Yok Mu*". Mr. Orhan, the director of the East African region of the organization, states that due to the Turkish interest in helping the Somalia and Dadaab refugee camps in Kenya, they provide some scholarships to students from those regions. He adds that the organization has a school building project estimated to be completed in 2013 in the Malindi district (in the Coast province of Kenya) which will accommodate more than 300 students. They preferred to attend Light Academy temporarily, until the project is completed (Orhan 9th August 2012)

However, Christian students think that those students are sponsored by the school itself, and the fact that there is a rapid increase in the Muslim population seems to support their argument. According to them, compared to previous years, the Muslim student rate of about 15% to 20 % has gone up to above 40% in the school.

According to the researcher, this could also be because of the Somali immigrants that have been increasing particularly in Nairobi. Since the Somali students cannot adapt easily to the Kenyan system due to particular subjects such Kiswahili, geography and history, they prefer the British system, which is relatively easier to adopt. Muslim administration and the freedom of Muslim practices could encourage them to prefer Light Academy to other schools. Mr. Abdillahi, a parent from a primary school in Nairobi, stated that most of his friends preferred Light Academy since administrators are Muslims; his son will not be exposed to other faiths (Abdillahi 18th June 2012).

In an assessment done with six students from both faiths, on 24th June, 2012, the students also argued that it is a common practice in schools not to conduct prayer during assemblies. Through in-depth interviews and assessments with teachers, the researcher found out that the way in which the assembly is held could easily determine who the administrators are. Most of the respondents who graduated from public schools expressed that their school allowed both Muslim and Christian prayers during assembly. Seemingly, the rest of the public schools had no Muslim prayer since Muslim students were very few. On the other hand, all respondents who had graduated from missionary schools reported that their schools had only one prayer, and that was according to its denomination. Minority schools and Muslim schools followed the same tradition. Ahmed, who graduated from one of the minority schools in Nairobi, said that both Muslims and Christians felt that the school did not respect their religion. However, they were studying in school for many reasons such as convenience of location, school fee and academic performance (Ahmed 26th May). The responses from private schools varied. According the researcher's observations, interviews and visits, the religious atmosphere of the private schools totally depends on the owner(s) of the school. Accordingly, Light Academy stands as a secular school since there is no prayer conducted during the assembly.

Figure 3: Respondents' opinions as to whether the school is religious or secular

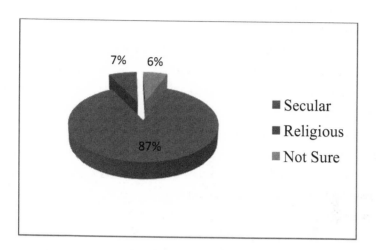

The majority of the respondents believed that Light Academy is a secular school. However, for many respondents the answers varied, and even contradicted each other. For example, those saying that it is secular wonder why the school places emphasis on moral values and accommodates and respects adherents from all faiths. Religious education is not a compulsory subject and is not covered in the national examination. On the other hand, those who were not sure testified that all students get equal opportunities and are even encouraged to worship freely, giving as an example the fact that Muslims can pray in one of the free rooms in the school, while Christians have Christian Union space in which to perform their religious obligations. Those saying it is religious explain that the school provides space to perform their religious activities when needed, and general moral values are taught and encouraged in school. The common criticism among those who interpreted Light Academy as a Muslim School was that while the school takes the Muslim students to *Jumna* prayer, Christian Students are not taken to church. Mr. Bilge admitted that Muslim students were taken to the mosque up until 2009. However, since that time, the prayer is being conducted in the school (Bilge 18th May). Mrs.

Elizabeth, the deputy, states that Christian students come from different denominations. Therefore, it is not possible to take each one to their particular church. However, she conducts a prayer with them on Fridays in the Christian Union meetings. The school also located a room for them for the Sunday services. One of the teachers conducts this service.

During an interview done with six students from both faiths, the researcher heard two criticisms from both parties. The Christians students' complaint was that the school does not provide them with a designated place for prayer, nor allow them to sing loudly, because administrators are Muslims. The Muslim criticism was similar; the school does not provide a prayer room; Muslims must use a multi-purpose room to perform their prayers. This room is also used to watch soccer and movies, and for many other activities. A prayer room should be only for prayer. In addition, they wanted to be able, at least once a week, to read *adhan*, the Muslims' loud call for prayer. However, they had not been given permission for that. After the discussion, the students realized that the school was at least behaving fairly in allowing students of both faiths to perform their prayer under the same conditions.

Figure 4: The percentage of the respondents' view as to whether the school is fair to other faiths or not

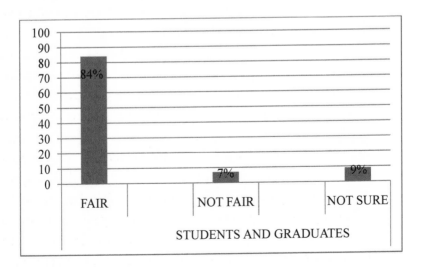

Students and graduates believed that the school is fair to both faiths. The rest of the respondents who believed that school is not fair mostly brought such arguments as shown above. In a FGD held on 20th June 2012, students were surprised to listen the same complaints from one other as shown above. They admitted that the school was indeed not inclined to favor any one religion.

98% of respondents agreed that Light Academy has given them an opportunity to socialize and interact freely with people from other faiths and cultures. 87% of parents interviewed said that parents' visits, open days, interfaith events and sending cards during the religious holidays contributed to mutual understanding. 98% of the interviewed graduates also acknowledged that the school allowed them to interact with students from other faiths, as it admits students from all faiths and cultures, and to some extent from all backgrounds, offering full and half scholarships to a few students.

According to the research, 86% of the students and graduates respect one another's faith and they feel respected in return. The rest of the respondents took it to be fair. There were no negative responses. 89% of the Christians know Muslims as fellow brothers who are guided by the Qur'an and have a different way of worshiping but they believe that they all worship the same God. On the other hand, 80% of the Muslim respondents believed that Christians are also believers like Muslims. They also described Christians as "The People of Book" as it is mentioned in Qur'an. However, in FGD of both faiths, students declared that a few years ago there were several students who called Christians *kefirs* (non-believers) or *natis* (dirty) but this behavior didn't last long. In response, the teachers addressed the issue through discussion with students.

During in-depth interviews with Turkish teachers 90% believed that Christians are "The People of Book" and 10% responded were not sure. 70% of the Kenyan teachers described Muslims as "believers like us". Consequently, the study shows that both Muslims and Christians have basic information about each other's faiths. Both Christians and Muslims take each other as believers of the same of God. Therefore, they have positive perceptions towards each other's faith. These perceptions promote positive relations among them.

3.5.1 Scholarships

Omeriye Foundation is a non-profit making organization. Even though Light Academy schools charge fees, these do not go to the Foundation or any individual, but are used to provide for the schools' expenses and scholarships. The schools offer scholarships to students from less fortunate families and to successful students (Osman 2nd August 2012). Data collected from the bursar indicates that out of 201 students studying in Kenya system 28 are under full scholarship, of which 24 are Christians while four are Muslims (Sakir 2nd July 2012). Seemingly, the administration follows a certain policy in giving scholarships, evaluating academic performance and family background. Religion is not considered.

3.5.2 The staff

Light Academy schools accommodate students from different ethnicity and faiths. According to the research, there are 26 ethnic groups learning in school out of the 42 known in Kenya. During the in-depth interviews and FGDs, teachers explain that the school is not selective according to peoples' faith or tribe. Private life is also not a concern of the school. However, in most of the other schools, teachers say, the picture is not the same. Quite a number of schools consider people's ethnicity, religion and private life. Almost all the religious schools prefer those who are from that denomination or faith. Many missionary schools also refuse to employ Muslim teachers. For instance, Mrs. Aisha recently applied to a Christian school for a vacant post as a teacher but asked if she can teach Christian values (Aisha 3rd July) since she is a Muslim.

The school has 52 teachers covering both the Kenyan and the British curriculum. Their percentages in terms of faith, Kenyan-Turkish teachers and ethnicity are as shown in the pie charts below;

Figure 5: Percentages of teachers' faith, ethnicity and Kenyan-Turkish

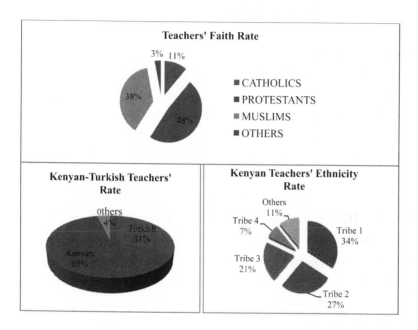

According to the study, the school has respect for all faiths and follows religious celebrations from both faiths alike. Mr. Mustafa, the headmaster of Mombasa primary, declares that they consider staffs' religious and cultural holidays when they arrange the annual leaves. The students also send cards to their parents during their respective holidays. It was reported that there is good feedback when the school sends card to Christian parents during the Easter holiday (Mustafa 17th May 2012). One of the parents, Mr. Mutuku, expressed that this shows how the school respects him as a Christian by celebrating his religious day with him (Mutuku 18th May 2012). Mr. Makambi, the staff manager in Boys' Secondary, and teacher Thomas from primary are Seventh Day Adventists and worship on Saturdays, official working days in Kenya. Following an appeal, Mr. Makambi is able to report to work on Sundays instead of Saturdays (Makambi 16th June 2012). Thomas has also been granted permission on Saturdays and it is not deducted from his annual leave (Thomas 6th June 2012). Both of them admit that they had difficulties in their former working places but they are very comfortable working in Light Academy and were surprised to get this privilege from a school whose almost all administrators are Muslims.

The study has also found that the Turkish teachers are very young (average age is 31.7). This could be both advantage and disadvantage. According to teacher Ismail, the deputy headmaster, young age is an advantage to the Turkish teachers. It makes communication easier since experience and social needs are almost the same in that age circle (Ismail 7th August 2012). On the other hand, some parents during the in-depth interviews took the young age as a disadvantage for academic experience. Some also observed that since Kenya is an English speaking country, language could be a barrier for some Turkish teachers. It takes time to learn the accent and improve their language due to their young age. However, seemingly, the teachers' dedication and commitment to teaching has led to the success of schools.

3.5.3 Implementation of Moral Values

According to Gülen, many people can teach but only a few can educate (2004: 208). During the study, the researcher observed that teaching and educating goes hand in hand at Light Academy schools. The school has unique activities in order to instill universal moral values in students through many social activities such as tea talks, sleepovers and parent visits, etc.... During in-depth interviews with teachers and parents, the researcher found out that those programs are unique. They promote peaceful co-existence and bringing mutual understanding among adherents of different faiths and cultures. Those activities, organized or hosted directly or indirectly, execute Gülen's ideas.

3.5.3.1 Tea Talks

These are extra activities organized by a class teacher or supervisor to bring students together. Students are grouped into small groups and each group gets an opportunity to join the optional tea talk at least once in a week. During these sessions, students sit together and are served tea and biscuits with their teacher. They are counseled and at the same time are reminded about school rules and their other responsibilities. According to Mr. Tumer, the deputy, moral issues are given priority during this time. Students are advised to live together as brothers and respect each other irrespective of their faith, background and community (Tumer 12th June 2012). Teacher Bulent also says that he reminds his students about moral values that are agreed by both Christianity and Islam. For example, stealing, cheating and abuse are discouraged in both religions, and he asks his students to quote relevant verses from their respective holy books to support this. He believes that by these discussions, they respect and even appreciate each other's faith (Bulent 14th July). On top of that, supervisors also organize tea talks at night for borders after the preparatory session ends.

More than 90% of all the respondents agreed that tea talks are useful. The topics most often discussed are respect, love, unity, mutual understanding, morality and academic progress. Although participant attendance is very high, the researcher observed that the current students take it as a social activity and that the opportunity to get together in a small group has more attraction than what is being discussed. However, the graduates feel the impact of those programs more. Abdullah and Barong says that most of students in their class were motivated to join tea talks not because of the agenda, but the chance to socialize with fellow friends and enjoy snacks and tea. These students cherish the outcome of these programs, as the life values discussed have helped them to live harmoniously with other people and to encourage them to embrace others in good conduct (Abdallah&Barongo 7th June 2012).

3.5.3.2 Sleepover Programs

These are programs created to bring together students (normally put into sizeable groups) such as day scholars, or weekly boarders. A letter is sent prior to the parents to ask them if they would allow their children to stay over the night or weekend in school. Teachers stay with the students and this give them more time with students at the personal level through playing games, and watching movies together. Some hours are set aside for studying in the subjects in which the students are weak. The students are encouraged to help each other and consult the teacher who acts as the supervisor in these programs when necessary.

Unlike other programs, sleepovers do not attract many students. For example, only 38%of all interviewees think they are useful. According to the researcher's observation, organizing these programs regularly is not that easy, particularly for married teachers, due to personal, family commitments and parent visits. On top of that, students mostly prefer spending weekends at school.

3.5.3.3 Parent Visits

This is a program organized to bring teachers, parents and students together. A parent is to be consulted before a visit through a letter or phone call, and asked if they are available. Teachers may visit the parent alone or in the company of their child and a few other classmates. These events take place at least once a year; thus a teacher has to sacrifice one of his evenings at least once a week to visit different parents.

Both teachers and parents get a chance to know each other as they discuss academic progress and character development of the student. A student forms a link between parent and teacher; hence good friendship is created, building and strengthening the Light Academy family.

96% of the interviewees agree that parent visits are very important. Most graduates expressed that parent visits have diversified their friendships and expanded their social lives. 81% of the interviewed graduates said that after parents' visits student teacher relations grow as a friendship triangle is developed. Most of the parents agree that they get an opportunity to socialize and interact with teachers and students from different backgrounds.

Mr. Mahammud's in-depth-interview tells us that he used to think *Iftar* was for the Muslim only and he could not invite anyone from other faiths to share with him, yet his religion teaches about sharing. However, through the parent visits he had learned to accommodate other people from different faiths and to confirm that nothing is as good as sharing *Iftar* together with other people (Mahammud 5th June 2012). Yet again, Mr. Peter adds that he used to be ignorant and relied on wrong information about Muslims; however through parents visits he has learned a lot and now respects Muslims (Peter 24th July 2012).

Mrs. Jane also shares that she enjoys when her son invites his fellow classmates from other faiths. She is very impressed with having prayers before the meal from both Muslim and Christian students. She adds that her son Kevin is always conscious of the kind of food his friends eat. She learned from him that, to Muslims, pork is not *Halal* (not allowed), among other foods, and she considers that when preparing the meal (Jane 24th July 2012).

Consequently, parent visits among other programs are the most dynamic and regular activity that brings people together and promotes respect among the different faiths and cultures.

3.5.4 Interfaith Events

The school organizes interfaith events and invites its parents for mutual understanding. During the month of *Ramadan*, in which Muslims fast, the school invites parents for *iftar* dinner. According to Mr. Veysel, the headmaster to primary in Nairobi, the purpose of those *iftar* events is to bring the parents together and at the same time to create respect and love to one another's faith as Light Academy family (Veysel 14th August 2012). Mr. John, a parent from Mombasa, was really excited when he heard of the invitation. It was the first time for him to be invited to such an event though he has been living among Muslims for a long time. He says this has really changed his attitudes towards the other faiths. He wonders why instead of dialogue we are in conflict (John 14th June 2012). Mr. Ali also admits that he has never thought of inviting non-Muslims, even his closest neighbors, to his home and to share his meal with them but now he realized the importance of a neighborhood that is about sharing no matter what religion (Ali 14th June 2012). Teacher Rachel, who has been working with the school for over 10 years, says this after attending *iftar* dinners:

> It is a unique style for a school to organize something like this, which manages to gather parents, teachers from different faiths. It promotes 'togetherness'. (Rachel 24 June 2012)

The school also hosts interfaith events once in a while in its auditorium that accommodates nearly 500 people per sitting. In 28 May 2011, an interfaith conference was held with the theme "Peaceful Co-existence and Gülen Movement". The speakers were invited from U.S. to share their experience and views on the theme. One of the speakers was Fr. Thomas Michel, the Head of Vatican's Pontifical Council for Interreligious Dialogue between1981-1994. The program brought students, graduates, teachers, parents and outsiders together. The most recent conference was held by Gülen Community in a hotel with the theme "Interfaith Dialogue for Peaceful Co-existence". The school also invited some parents, particularly those who are academicians and government officials. Mrs. Opiyo, who was one of the participants, shared her opinion:

> "When my children went through Light Academy, I knew that there was something very special and very good about the school, but I did not know exactly what it was until this conference" (Opiyo 5th June 2012).

The school is involved under the Omeriye Foundation in distributing meat to all its staff and outsiders, regardless of their religion, during *EidhulAdha*, the Muslim festival of sacrifice. During the in-depth interviews, the staff has expressed appreciation to school administration for being considered though they are not Muslims. Tr. Nancy, the deputy in primary Nairobi, stated that she has learned from Muslims to share, and this creates love toward one another in the neighborhood (Nancy 27th July 2012).

The schools are playing an important role in the promotion of mutual understanding between the adherents of both religions. The respondents have shown high appreciation for those programs. Therefore, the establishments of those schools serve not only to educate the students but also to serve the society in which they are set.

3.6 The Impact of the Schools on Students

Many schools in Kenya are run directly or indirectly according to Christian-based values. Because of that, the Muslim community in Kenya was reluctant to seek secular education for their children, fearing that they would not be given equal opportunities. Thus, Gülen-inspired schools provide an environment in which Muslims can interact with others without fear of losing their faith and identity, since the school is not inclined to any religion. In addition, Muslim students can easily practice their religion without any interference. A FGD done with 5 Muslim students on 1st July indicated that some of the students interpret the school as a Muslim school because its administration allows them to practice their religion freely. They agreed that it is rare to get a high school offering such freedom, apart from Muslim schools.

The study has also shown that school is a bridge between Christianity and Islam since it promotes mutual understanding and avoids misconceptions. Abdul, a graduate, says he was brought up in the remote parts of Garissa where there were no Christians. He was taught that Christians were *najis* (dirty) and Muslims were not to eat from the same plate with Christians and that Muslims had to take a bath whenever touched by Christians. Thus, he was made to understand Christians as less-than-human. It happened that he had to join his high school in Light Academy and, unfortunately, for him, he was the only Muslim student in his stream-form 1A. He recalls when he was in an examination room and he needed to sharpen his pencil. His Christian desk mate had a sharpener but he felt that he could not use it. Sometimes he had no notes, but believed he could not ask from his classmates. He later learned that Christians are also believers like Muslims. Now he applauds Light Academy for taking the responsibility to discuss religious problems and difficulties in order to reach to a common understanding (Abdul 25th July 2012).

Similarly, Robert, a graduate, shared his experience. He used to hate all Muslims with passion and, to him, Islam and terrorism were inseparable. This belief was due to his father's killing in the 1998 U.S. Bomb blast in Nairobi. Only after enrollment in Light Academy and reading a few of Gülen's articles, did he distinguish between Islam and terrorism and came to learn that terrorists cannot be believers though many terrorists claim to be Muslims. According to him, he met the peaceful Islam in the school (Robert 12th June 2012). It seems that Light Academy Schools play an important role on eradicating people's misconceptions about other's faith.

3.7 General Overview of Other Schools in Kenya

The general perception of the schools in Kenya is as Public, Private and Religious schools. According to the researcher, two particular groups could be added:

Minority schools that are run by a particular nation but enroll other students. Those schools particularly belong to Asian-origin Kenyans and foreigners.

Public sponsored religious schools: Those schools are mostly built by the government. Sponsors have a central role to play in terms of hiring of teachers and staff. The teachers are paid by the government, and sponsors collect the fees to run the school based on their perspective. While the actual owner of the school is the government, the school is managed by the sponsors in return for their sponsorship and investment.

During in-depth interviews and two FGDs done with total of 14 teachers on 4th August, the researcher found that the religious environment of the school depends on who runs the school. Thus, the religious atmosphere of a school is very much associated with its owner. All the respondents graduated from public schools expressed that their schools were fair to all faiths. Students were allowed to join in their prayers freely. While nearly half of them were offering IRE, unlike missionary schools CRE was optional. According to researcher's investigations, not all the public schools are able to offer IRE due to the shortage of IRE teachers or low number of Muslim students in the school. For instance, Mrs. Munyafu, the tutor in Westland District in Nairobi, asked Supreme Council of Kenyan Muslims' assistance to get an IRE teacher for one of the schools in her district but no one has responded in the last one year (Munyafu 31th May 2012). It appears that public schools are trying their best in terms of being fair to all faiths.

On the contrary, the religious and minority schools differ from public schools. Most of the respondents who studied in missionary schools interviewed stated that CRE was compulsory. In addition, most of them were conducting the prayers according to their faith and forcing others to follow exactly that.

Similarly, a large majority of the Muslim schools do not accommodate other faiths since they strictly follow Islamic regulations and offer Islamic subjects as compulsory. Thus, those schools are isolated from other faiths and do not allow their students to interact with them. The coast province has more schools compared to other parts of Kenya, but very few Christian students study in those schools. The Muslim headscarf may also be part of the uniform, thus few Christian girls attend Muslim schools.

Some of the private missionary schools enroll students only from their faith. Those schools also isolate themselves from other faiths and therefore do not create opportunities for religious and cultural interaction. Teacher Mary, who studied in such a school in her primary and secondary education, expressed that in her university she experienced difficulties interacting with Muslims, Hindus and other denominations. She felt as if she had been indoors for a long time but now met the real life. She felt lucky joining a public university rather than a religious one (Mary 5th August 2012). The researcher witnessed similar statements from Muslims before this study. Some people who study in Muslim schools might also have difficulties in interacting with other faiths. Thus, we can see that religious schools are isolated and do not allow social interaction with other faiths.

Public sponsored schools have a different position among other schools in Kenya. The students select those schools by taking into consideration their grades, proximity and ranking of the school. Some students may find the best public school is in his or her hometown but is sponsored by a religious group. There is no big difference in terms of management between sponsored and private religious schools. Many respondents feel that the government is doing more for the public sponsored schools than for the private religious schools. It is felt by some that the government gives preference to particular faiths or denominations over others. Missionary schools are the ones who are the beneficiaries of this system as compared to Muslims since there are more missionary schools than Muslim schools.

According to FGDs done with teachers and in-depth interviews, a majority of respondents whose faith or denomination was compromised believe that they developed a negative attitude towards that particular school and the faith or religion with which they were affiliated. This attitude is much stronger among Muslim respondents, and could even turn into hatred. The conversion takes place often. Seemingly, those schools either convert or create in students' heart negative attitudes towards other faiths or denomination.

Most religious-biased schools are not accommodative to other faith and denominations. Other schools could also be inclined to favor a particular religion or denomination according to its administration's will. Public schools are more neutral than other schools in Kenya. This neutral atmosphere is a result of the natural freedom in public schools. In Light Academy, this neutral atmosphere is evident and is much more advanced than in many other schools.

Gülen-inspired schools have a different concept compared to many other schools in Kenya. Although they are run by Turkish Sunni Muslims, they accommodate students, teachers and staff from all faiths and ethnic groups and seem to be fair to all. There is freedom of worship and thus a promotion of mutual understanding. Their graduates have positive attitudes towards one another's faith.

4.1 Conclusion

Gülen-inspired schools are trying to create a new generation based on universal religious values which would create mutual understanding amongst adherents of different faiths and cultures. In this manner Gülen is not only calling people towards interfaith dialogue but also bringing up a generation that is already living in dialogue. The schools inspired by his educational and dialogue ideas are established to bring about a civilization of love among the people of different faiths and cultures. Education is a common language to bring people together for this very purpose.

Gülen's theory of education and dialogue is implemented by way of programs such as sleepovers, tea talks and parent visits. Other activities include the organizing of interfaith events and *iftar* dinners and inviting parents and many other adherents of different faiths to share their religious knowledge thereby creating peaceful co-existence amongst people of various faiths. Through the establishment of those schools not only are students educated, they are also taught to serve the society in which they originate.

Public schools are trying to be fair to all faiths while most of the religious schools and minority schools favor a particular faith or denomination to others. Students who have to study in a majority of such schools do so due to the schools' academic performance, proximity or competitive school fees but there is neglect in terms of their religious demands and in many instances there is coercion to worship according to the school administration's belief. In return either students convert or grow to dislike that particular faith and this becomes a barrier to interfaith dialogue.

Public sponsored religious schools also favor particular faiths or denominations by using government funds. Missionary schools are the main beneficiaries of this system as compared to Muslim faith schools due to their disproportionate number. Some denominations end up having more schools than others. For these types of schools, the government favors missionaries of particular denominations over others.

The religious atmospheres of the private schools in Kenya totally depend on the owner of the school. On the other hand, religious-biased schools are not accommodative to other faiths and denominations. Public schools are more neutral compared to other schools in Kenya. This neutral atmosphere is a result of freedom that is natural in public schools. This neutral atmosphere is desired in Light Academy and is therefore planned and controlled, hence the Academy is more advanced in this regard than many other schools.

Consequently, Gülen-inspired schools are secular but encourage the practice of different religious beliefs. They enroll students and recruit teachers and staff from different faiths. They employ unique methods of educating society by using universally-adhered to values which promote mutual understanding. People who study and work in these schools have positive and constructive relationships towards one another's faith. This study also demonstrates how a school could be secular and at the same time encourage religion and fairness to all. Therefore, Gülen-inspired schools provide an alternative to religion-biased schools in Kenya and promote positive and constructive Christian-Muslim relations in Kenya.

Bibliography

Books

Baur, John. *2000 Years of Christianity in Africa*. 2nd. Nairobi: Pauliness, 2009.

Kahumbi, Maina. "Christian-Muslim Relations in Kenya." In *Islam in Kenya*, edited by Suleyman Bakari and Saad Yahya. Nairobi: Mewa, 1995.

Bulletins

FridayBulletin. *The Friday Bulletin: The Weekly Muslim News Update* (The Jamia Mosque Committee), no. 261 (February 2007): 1.

Websites

Light Academy. 2012. http://www.lightacademy.ac.ke/?content, nSLFB ChiKl2gi9g (accessed July 2012, 2012).

LightAcademy. *www.lightacademy.ac.ke*. February 19th, 2011. http://www.lightacademy.ac.ke/mombasasecondary/?news,XTILPQul GBifojG (accessed August 11, 2012). fgulen. *fethullahgulen.org*. Fethullah Gulen Website. 2010. http://www.fethullahgulen.org/about-fethullah-gulen/introducing-fethullah-gulen.html (accessed March 22, 2012). *http://en.fgulen.com*. March 15th, 2012. http://en.fgulen.com/about-fethullah-gulen/introducing-fethullah-gulen (accessed March 15, 2012).

Interviews

Abdallah&Barongo. Nairobi, 7th June 2012.

Abdillahi. 18th June 2012.

Abdul. Nairobi, 25th July 2012.

Abdul, Jabir. (July 18, 2012).

Adan. Nairobi, 26th July 2012.

Ahmed. Nairobi, 26th May.

Aisha. Nairobi, 3rd July.

Akkilic. Nairobi, 29th July 2012.

Ali. Mombasa, 14th June 2012.

Altindis. Mombasa, 14th June 2012.

Bilge. Nairobi, 18th May.

Bulent. Nairobi, 14th July.

Calvin. Nairobi, 31th July 2012.

Engin. Nairobi, 13th July 2012.

Gurhan. Nairobi, 29th May 2012.

Ismail. Nairobi, 7th August 2012.

Jabir. Nairobi, 18th July 2012.

Jane. Nairobi, 24th July 2012.

John. Mombasa, 14th June 2012

Joseph. Nairobi, 15th June 2012.

Mahammud. Nairobi, 5th June 2012.

Mahmut. Nairobi, 26th July 2012.

Makambi. 16th June 2012.

Mark&Zoram&Ali. Nairobi, 12th July 2012.

Mary. Nairobi, 5th August 2012.

Mehmet. Nairobi, 15th May 2012.

Mr.Ali. Mombasa, 14th June 2012.

Mr.John. Nairobi, 22nd July 2012.

Mr.Makambi. 16th June 2012.

Mr.Mustafa. Mombasa, 17th May 2012.

Mr.Mutuku. Mombasa, 18th May 2012.

Mrs.Jane. Nairobi, 24th July 2012.

Mrs.Opiyo. Nairobi, 5th June 2012.

Munyafu. Nairobi, 31th May 2012.

Mustafa. Mombasa, 17th May 2012.

Mutuku. Mombasa, 18th May 2012.

Mwangi. Nairobi, 12th June 2012.

Nancy. Nairobi, 27th July 2012.

Opiyo. Nairobi, 5th June 2012.

Orhan. Nairobi, 9th August 2012.

Osman. Nairobi, 2nd August 2012.

Otieno. Nairobi, 21th May 2012.

Paul. Nairobi, 17th June 2012.

Peter. Nairobi, 24th July 2012.

Rachel. Nairobi, 24 th June 2012

Robert. Nairobi, 12th June 2012.

Sakir. Nairobi, 2nd July 2012.

Thomas. Nairobi, 6th June 2012.

Tumer. Nairobi, 12th June 2012.

Tunc&Were. Nairobi, 2nd July 2012.

Veysel. Nairobi, 14th August 2012.

Addendum: Bridging the Divide

The divide between Somalia, Kenya and the United states has been almost insurmountable for refugees who fled the violence of Somalia for refugee camps in Kenya and then were able to migrate to the United States and settle in the Minneapolis area where most Somali Americans now live. One of the unique success stories is Ilhan Omar, a 34-year-old Muslim woman immigrant from Somalia who crossed from Somalia in 1991 with her family to a Mombasa, Kenya refugee camp where she remained for four years until she and her family were allowed to immigrate to the USA. In 1995 she and her family moved to Minneapolis where she pursued her education earning a degree in political science from North Dakota State University and also becoming involved in local politics among the Somali community in Minneapolis. She began her professional career as a Community Nutrition Educator with the University of Minnesota from 2006 to 2009 working in the Greater Minneapolis area. During this time Ilhan began her career in local politics and became campaign manager for Andrew Johnson who won his election to the Minneapolis City Council. Ilhan then served as his Senior Policy Aide from 2013 to 2015. In September of 2015 she became Director of Policy and Initiatives for the Woman Organizing Women's Network. In 2016 she became the first Somali American woman to win an election as a state representative in Minnesota.

On Nov. 8, (2016) Ilhan Omar made history when she was elected the first Somali-American lawmaker in the U.S.

"My election win offers a counter-narrative to the bigotry in the world," Minnesota State Representative-elect Omar, 34, says in the new issue of PEOPLE. "This is a land of immigrants, and most come here for opportunity, a second chance. It's our time to fight for the America we know we can have."

(http://people.com/politics/ilhan-omar-first-somali-american-legislator-counter-narrative-to-bigotry/)

Just as the story of Barak Obama, of Kenyan ancestry, gave Americans an opportunity to bridge the racial divide in the United States during his rise to the American presidency, Ilhan Omar represents a new generation of East African immigrants who can overcome the stereotyping that has informed so much of the 2016 presidential election. American Muslims can find in her a new role model for integration into the US democratic political system which can be beneficial not just for the USA but for the entire world.

(https://www.ilhanomar.com/)

Select Bibliography

Armstrong, Karen, *History of God*. New York: Ballantine, 1993.

Armstrong, Karen, *The Battle for God*. New York: Alfred Knopf, 2000.

Armstrong, Karen, *Fields of Blood: Religion and the History of Violence*. New York: Alfred Knops, 2014.

Bulliet, Richard, *The Case for Islamo-Christian Civilization*. New York: Columbia University Press, 2004.

Cetin, Muhammed, *The Gulen Movement: Civic Service Without Borders*. New York: Blue Dome Press: 2010.

Cook, Steven, *The Struggle for Egypt: From Nasser to Tahrir Square*. Oxford: Oxford University Press, 2012.

Dardres, George, and Marvin L. Krier Mich, *In the Spirit of St. Francis and the Sultan: Catholics and Muslims Working Together for the Common God*. Maryknoll, New York: Orbis Books, 2011.

Esposito, John L., *The Future of Islam*. Oxford: Oxford University Press, 2010.

Esposito, John L., editor, *The Oxford History of Islam*. Oxford: Oxford University Press, 1999.

Gerges, Fawaz, A., *A History of ISIS*. Princeton, New Jersey: Princeton University Press

Grudzen, Gerald, *Medical Theory About the Body and Soul in the Middle Ages: The First Western Medical Curriculum*. Lewiston, New York: Edwin Mellen Press, 2007

Grudzen, Gerald and Shamsur Rahman, *Spirituality and Science: Greek, Judeo-Christian and and Islamic Perspectives*. Bloomington, Indiana: Author House, second edition, 2014.

Grudzen, Gerald and John Raymaker, *Steps* Toward *Vatican III: Catholics Pathfinding a Global Spirituality with Islam and Buddhism.* Lanham, Maryland: University Press of America, 2008.

Gulen, Fethullah, *The Essential of the Islamic Faith.* Clifton, New Jersey: Tughra Books, 2011

Huntington, Samuel, *The Clash of Civilizations and the Remaking of the World Order.*

Kelsey, *Arguing the Just War in Islam.* Cambridge: Harvard University Press, 2007.

Kung, Hans, trans. John Bowden, *Islam: Past, Present and Future.* Oxford: One World, 2007.

Maher, Shiraz, *Salafi-Jihadism, The History of an Idea.* Oxford: Oxford University Press, 2016.

Mvumbi, Frederik Ntedika, OP, editor, *Interfaith Dialogue: Towards a Culture of Working Together.* Nairobi, Kenya: Catholic University of East Africa, 2009.

Mvumbi, Frederic Ntedica, OP, *Journey into Islam: An Attempt to Awaken Christians in Africa.* Nairobi, Kenya: Paulines, 2008.

Raymaker, John and Gerald Grudzen with Joe Holland, *Spiritual Paths to an Ethical and Ecological Global Civilization.* Washington, D.C.: Pacem in Terris Press, 2013

Raymaker, John, *Bernard Lonergan's Third Way of the Heart and Mind: Bridging Some Buddhist-Christian-Muslim-Secularist Misunderstandings with a Global Security Ethics.* Lantham, Maryland: Hamilton Books, 2016.

Weiss, Michael and Hassan Hassan, *ISIS: Inside the Army of Terror.* New York: Regan Arts, 2015.

Index

Marita Grudzen with members of our
Mombasa Interfaith Educational Training Team.

Made in the USA
San Bernardino, CA
12 June 2019